THE ENIGMA SPY

an autobiography

THE ENIGMA SPY

THE STORY OF THE MAN WHO CHANGED THE COURSE OF WORLD WAR TWO

By John Cairncross

Century · London

Published by Century in 1997

1 3 5 7 9 10 8 6 4 2

First published in the United Kingdom in 1997 by Century
Random House UK Limited
20 Vauxhall Bridge Road, London SW1V 2SA

Random House Australia (Pty) Limited
20 Alfred Street, Milsons Point, Sydney,
New South Wales 2061, Australia

Random House New Zealand Limited
18 Poland Road, Glenfield
Auckland 10, New Zealand

Random House South Africa (Pty) Limited
Endulini, 5a Jubilee Road, Parktown 2193, South Africa

Random House UK Limited Reg. No. 954009

A CIP catalogue record for this book is available from the British Library

Papers used by Random House UK Limited are natural, recyclable products made from wood grown in sustainable forests. The manufacturing processes conform to the environmental regulations of the country of origin

ISBN 0 7126 7884 0

Printed and bound in the United Kingdom by
Mackays of Chatham plc, Chatham, Kent

CONTENTS

Acknowledgements

I would like in John's name to thank his many friends and colleagues all over the world who encouraged him to write this book and who have waited patiently for its publication

There are also those who after John's death have helped to bring his story to the public. These include my friend Stephen Shotnes of Simons Muirhead & Burton, and my astute legal advisor Andrew Best who acted as my consultant and literary agent, wielding from time to time his magic pen in an editorial capacity. My personal thanks go to Mark Booth for recognising the merits of John's story and gently yet authoritatively guiding its production. Thanks also to Liz Rowlinson and the sympathetic team at Random House who, at every stage have taken into consideration the circumstances that have attended the publication of this book.

Sir Alec Cairncross and his wife Mary have been a source of personal strength to me following John's death. I greatly appreciate Alec's unflagging support of his brother's right to go public with his version of events and his assistance in the preparation of this book. I am most grateful to Richard Norton-Taylor for his help and encouragement as well for his Introduction. My brother Robert Brinkerhoff who knew John well, was personally and professionally a shoulder to lean on.

Finally, I owe an immense debt of gratitude to Ronnie Challoner for his work in editing John's manuscript. He has championed this project from its outset as John's advocate, lending to it his invaluable knowledge of history and of the Intelligence Services.

Gayle Cairncross

Preface

This is the first and only account by my younger brother John that I have ever been given of his contacts with the Soviet Union. During his lifetime he maintained a rigorous silence about those contacts and at no time confided in me. Even when I wrote to him in 1964 after hearing officially, to my utter astonishment, that he had been a Soviet agent, I received no reply or comment. Nor did he indicate to me at any time in later years the part he had played. I was not aware that he was bound to silence under the agreement reached with MI5 in 1964. In accordance with that agreement, he remained silent even when the most extra-ordinary charges were levelled against him and when former members of the KGB added testimony which the authorities must have known were without foundation, but which they left uncontradicted. As the accusations multiplied, however, he felt impelled to write his own account of his activities and had completed a draft of his book sometime before his return to England, where he died in October 1995.

John was a truthful person, highly intelligent, but with strong views of his own. These views are given full expression in this book and have to be understood before any final judgement is made of his conduct. Personally, I find his account entirely convincing. I am deeply grateful to Ronnie Challoner and John's wife Gayle who edited John's hand and typewritten drafts. It is largely due to Gayle's tenacity that this book is being published.

Contrary to what is often asserted, John was never a member of the Communist Party and was no admirer of the Soviet régime, although he did for a time associate with members of the party during his two years as a student at Cambridge. He was, however, very much alive to the importance of an understanding with the Soviet Union in the face of the growing military power of Germany. Few people today appreciate how grim was the international outlook in the late 1930s under a government that went to extraordinary lengths, and persevered for an extraordinary time, in an effort to appease a Germany arming for war. Like many young men of his generation, he had no confidence in the policies of his government. Not only did the Chamberlain administration do nothing to check the growing military power of Germany when it was still possible, but seemed content to let Hitler attack Russia unimpeded (if he so chose), ignoring the obvious risk that if Russia was subdued it would not be long before Britain too was brought under the control of the Nazis. If Britain was to survive with any semblance of independence, its best hope was to make common cause with Russia, the only power capable of withstanding a German assault. Helping the USSR in those circumstances could be an act of patriotism, as it became in June 1941.

John was particularly upset by the accusation that he had been an atom spy. The only evidence, as he points out, is that his name appeared by mistake on the minutes of a meeting which he did not attend and in whose business he took no part. He was also indignant at being labelled the 'Fifth Man' or one of the 'Ring of Five'. That he knew Blunt, Burgess, Maclean and Philby has never been in question; but that he knew that any one of them was a Soviet spy until it was publicly disclosed he strenuously denied. The 'Ring of Five' appears to have been a phrase used by the Russians in 1943 to bring under one heading the agents to whom they felt particularly indebted. No link has been established between John and the others and there is no evidence of any cooperation with them or knowledge of what the others were doing. He insists that he acted on his own and for his own reasons. What he did was never aimed at damaging what he saw as the interests of the United Kingdom but at contributing to the defeat of the Nazis.

The discovery of papers written by John in Burgess's trunk is generally taken to imply collaboration with Burgess in passing information to Moscow, but there is no truth in this; he was taken aback just as much as others by the unmasking of Burgess in 1951 and had understood that the papers were destined for a secret British department for which Burgess worked.

Not much is known about what specific information John did transmit. He handed over no papers until September 1938, was moved from the Foreign Office to the Treasury three months later – and so had no access to Foreign Office material – and he was, with one exception, completely inactive between the departure of his handler to Moscow in February 1939 and the entry of Russia into the war on the Allied side in June 1941. With Russia as an ally, he reassessed his position with the KGB and came to a deliberate decision while at Bletchley Park to become an agent for the duration of the war. He gave the Russians what help he could, taking a calculated risk that the Government was not prepared to take. What he transmitted in 1943 is now known to have included intercepts of German radio messages that were of critical importance to the USSR in what proved to be the decisive battle at Kursk on the Eastern Front. In doing so he ran the risk that his action might reveal to the Germans that their cipher system had been broken but he judged, rightly as it proved, that the Russians would show diligent regard for secrecy.

Before the war John had been a somewhat reluctant agent, with little regard for the Soviet Union, but taking a long view of the potential value of links to the one country that he judged capable of holding out against German expansionism. During the war, once the USSR had become our ally he saw the possibility of supplying information of real value to them. When the war was over he continued in a desultory fashion, presumably afraid of the consequences of a categorical break with the KGB and preferring to let his association with the KGB wither away. As a junior Treasury official, anything he could tell the Russians was of minor importance. However, stories have appeared in recent years implying that after 1948 a new Soviet handler, Yuri Modin, succeeded in reviving John's usefulness as a source of military information. He is, for example, alleged to have supplied information on the military expenditure of the Western powers and provided details of the responsibilities of his Treasury colleagues.

John insisted that everything alleged about his post-war activities was pure fabrication, and that there was no renewed burst of activity on his part as an agent after Modin's arrival. Modin had every temptation to embroider his account, especially as the truth was simple and dull: throughout the post-war years the information John supplied was of little interest to the USSR.

What sort of person was John Cairncross? As a young man he had studied at Glasgow, in Paris at the Sorbonne, and at Cambridge. He was a brilliant linguist and, had he found academic employment in 1936 he would have had a long and distinguished career as a scholar. His two years in Paris in 1933–4 and two long bicycle tours on the continent that he made by himself in those years helped to develop his self-reliance and informality. He was something of a loner and very much an intellectual: widely-read, unconventional, never well-off. He shared with one brother an interest in Shakespeare, and an interest in economics with another.

He was always ready to challenge authority and in his conversation this manifested itself in a certain arrogance. He was often informative and entertaining, but at times he became argumentative and sometimes prickly. We got on better with one another when our contacts were not too prolonged.

It was his misfortune, as he acknowledges in this book, to have passed top of the entrance examination into the Foreign Office and so attracted the attention of the KGB. He was not really fitted for a diplomatic career, least of all one assuming ample means, but was attracted by the idea of a career involving long spells abroad. He had little reason to regret that he was moved out of the Foreign Office after two years, or even that he was obliged to leave the Civil Service altogether in 1952, whatever the financial and other difficulties to which that exposed him.

Fundamentally he was a man of letters, a scholar and a poet, not a man of affairs. For most of his life after 1952 he was able to give himself to what he most excelled in and most enjoyed. In that time he embarked on a new career and built up an international reputation as an authority on French literature of the seventeenth century. He wrote three books on Molière, translated into English verse plays by Racine and Corneille, the Fables of La Fontaine and poems in many different languages and in addition produced poetry of his own. Among his other publications was an original and highly entertaining account of polygamy in the West from the sixteenth century onwards. What most fascinated him throughout his life was the emergence of modern ways of thinking in seventeenth-century France. Although he never produced the development of this perception, it would have been his crowning in intellectual achievement

Sir Alec Cairncross
Oxford, 1997

Introduction

John Cairncross was one of the most gifted young men of his generation, a brilliant linguist and scholar and most unlikely spy. He will go down in history as the man who helped the Russians win the Battle of Kursk in the summer of 1943, the largest tank battle in history and a crucial turning point in the Second World War. According to the Russian writer Genrikh Borovik, Cairncross helped save 'the lives of tens of thousands' by providing the Russians, while he was posted at the Government Code and Cipher School (GC&CS) at Bletchley Park, with ENIGMA decrypts giving details of *Luftwaffe* formations. Russia was able to destroy 500 German bombers before the battle, thus paving the way to Hitler's defeat on the Eastern front. For this Moscow is reported to have awarded Cairncross *in absentia* the Order of the Red Banner.

I first met the former spy and respected authority on Molière in 1991, a few months after he was 'exposed' by Christopher Andrew and Oleg Gordievsky in their book *KGB: The Inside Story* as the 'Fifth Man' and the 'first atom spy'. The excited media commentary had led me to expect a shady, slippery individual living in opulence in the French Provençal countryside. Instead, I met a wiry and soft-spoken Scotsman, ascetic in appearance, clearly an intellectual, living in a modest rented house with his partner, Gayle, and her three Salukis hounds. He was eager to respond to Andrew's and Gordievsky's assertions and give his own account of events. 'I have been stamped (such is the power of stereotypes) as a leftist,' he told me. 'Patriotism and defence of democracy are obviously not sufficient grounds for helping an ally against Hitler.' When Neville Chamberlain and his policy of appeasement came up during our conversations he became passionately agitated as he remembered those dark days. 'My contribution to the Russians,' he said, 'was pro-Allied and not anti-British.'

But when would this independent-minded Scotsman who had acted against the wishes of his government present his story to the public? He believed he was still bound to silence by a mutual agreement with MI5, which they had offered him after his full debriefing in 1964. At that time silence had been convenient to all concerned, especially to Anthony Blunt who, as part of a deal granting him immunity from prosecution, had shopped John Cairncross. So, while Blunt and others were protected, Cairncross was abandoned to a life of uncertainty, the status of his immunity remaining unclear, and when it was in their interest to do so, the security and intelligence agencies broke their side of the agreement concerning confidentiality by leaking partial or mendacious material to selected writers. Perhaps Cairncross was a victim of his own naiveté, for it took him a long time to defy the authorities and decide to publish his own account which criticises British Intelligence for their handling of his case. Has he the right to tell his own story? I certainly believe he does, just as the public has a right to know it.

Meanwhile, *KGB: The Inside Story* was comprehensively savaged by espionage experts and the press. Defector Gordievsky's reliability as a source was increasingly called into question as his assertions against Cairncross were scrutinised. He acknowledged that he had not seen the Cairncross file and, even though he had written the history of the KGB's operations in Britain, he admitted he had no documentary evidence to back up his claim that Cairncross was the 'Fifth Man'. He said that the claim was based on 'people in the KGB talking openly about Cairncross'. Andrew's and Gordievsky's other 'revelation' was that 'the first warning of the Anglo-American decision to build an atomic bomb probably came from John Cairncross'. They based their claim on a single official document which lists, by a clerical error, Cairncross as Joint Secretary to the Scientific Advisory Committee chaired by Lord Hankey, cabinet minister without portfolio.

Nevertheless *KGB: The Inside Story*, which had been vetted by the Security and Intelligence establishment, was enthusiastically welcomed by among others Lord Armstrong, the former Cabinet Secretary. He seized on it as proof that Roger Hollis, the former head of MI5, had not been – as a group of MI5 molehunters, notably Peter Wright, had maintained – a Soviet agent. Armstrong concluded that the debate about whether there was a 'Superspy' in the agency was now ended and the allegations against Hollis refuted. The quasi-official sponsorship in 1990 of Cairncross's 'outing' suggests that MI5 was, indeed, still worried about the nagging uncertainty of earlier Soviet penetration of the agency. Thus the debate about the 'Fifth Man' was conveniently confused by the establishment with the entirely separate search for a Supermole in MI5. But, as John Cairncross convincingly shows in this book, the allegations over continuing Soviet penetration of MI5 were never related to the activities of the so called 'Ring of Five'. MI5 spycatchers were after another mole and the ultimately inconclusive investigation on the part of the FLUENCY Committee, set up to look into these internal matters, confirms that the case is still open.

Cairncross's moving story is set against the background of pre-war Britain; a most dramatic and turbulent period in British history. It personifies the acute dilemma facing a generation deeply disillusioned by the policies of a government which turned a blind eye to the Nazis and the rise of Fascism in Europe.

At the age of twenty-three John Cairncross was trapped into a meeting with his first controller, Otto. The unworldly scholar, more at home with French literature than the murky world of espionage and counter-espionage, but with a powerful intellect and a particular Scottish tenacity, attempted to pursue his own independent line. Whether he is seen as an anti-hero or an impressionable youth – a tragic victim of circumstance, his decision even today will create debate about those issues where duty and private conscience come into conflict. The reader will ask what he or she might have done in a similar situation. Cairncross himself says he can be accused of 'recklessness, arrogance and naiveté' in believing it possible to find his own way through the world of the KGB where intrigue, deliberate distortion, and half-truths thrive. This unclubbable loner, more suited to an academic life, who entered the Foreign Office after coming top of both the Civil Service and Diplomatic Service exams (an unparalleled achievement) was uncomfortable with the old boy network. He was also at odds with the policies of Whitehall and its culture of appeasement. He believed that the 'authorities would recoil in horror' were he to report the KGB's approach and that he was certain to be dismissed from the service and unlikely to find another job. Although his 'survival instincts' in part made him temporise with the KGB, he insists that he was never prepared to cooperate fully with them.

He readily acknowledges that there was a certain inappropriateness in his accepting, from time to time, small sums of money from Otto, who resembled a European intellectual rather than a KGB handler, but Cairncross did not spy for money. His critics say he betrayed one of Britain's priceless secrets – that Bletchley Park was routinely intercepting and decoding Germany's communications. Cairncross agonised over whether he should provide raw ENIGMA intelligence to the Russians but decided that not to do so would be morally unjustifiable.

Cairncross always operated alone. Although he knew them socially, he was never in league with Philby, Blunt, Maclean and Burgess. Indeed, the significance of Moscow's use of the phrase 'Ring of Five' has been hugely exaggerated. As far as the KGB was concerned, it was a useful concept denoting those who had provided particularly valuable information. It also had tremendous propaganda value and was useful to the KGB as a means of self-congratulation. Borovik said in his book *The Philby Files*, published in 1994, that Yuri Modin, the KGB agent in London and Cairncross's last 'controller', told him that he uses the term the 'Ring of Five' very conditionally. 'There was so much espionage information coming out of England [during the war] that we could barely handle it at the centre. We had to give priority to someone. So we chose five of the most valuable ones. The make-up of those five changed from time to time, depending on the effectiveness or workplace of an agent at a specific time.' Modin added: 'I never included Cairncross in the Five, even though he was a valuable agent and stood out.' In the English version of his autobiography *My Five Cambridge Friends*, also published in 1994, Modin says that in 1944 'Cairncross was added to the four agents to whose cases I had been assigned. He was the "fifth man".' Yet, the original French edition of the book does not use the term and Modin later denied he had ever used it.

There are other claims and counter-claims. In 1994, an Australian writer, Roland Perry, wrote another version of this running controversy, simply called *The Fifth Man*, claiming the title really belonged to Lord (Victor) Rothschild. He wrote the book after extensive interviews with Modin in Moscow. Modin told him – and Modin repeated this to me later – that Cairncross gave him valuable details of preparations, in the late 1940s, to set up NATO, a charge significantly never made by Andrew and Gordievsky. Modin also says in his book that Cairncross told him the allies 'were capable of producing a device on uranium 235'.

When I asked Modin only this year, 1997, if Cairncross had supplied atomic secrets to Moscow, as Andrew and Gordievsky had claimed, Modin replied: 'He had no opportunity.' These claims are also dismissed by other former KGB officers as 'rubbish'. In fact, Modin's claim that Cairncross continued to pass Moscow valuable secrets after the war is not substantiated by any documentary evidence. Indeed, there were those in Moscow who suspected from the kind of information Cairncross was supplying that he was a double agent.

Cairncross vehemently denied all Modin's claims and dismissed his book as pure fantasy. But by the time it appeared, Cairncross had suffered a debilitating stroke, preventing him from confronting the accusations in this book as he was able to face down the unsubstantiated charges of Andrew and Gordievsky. Sadly he died before his autobiography saw the light of day but he was, at the age of eighty-three, prepared to face public scrutiny and defend everything he had written, demanding only that the Security Services be made more accountable to the public.

Cairncross's only reason for coming forward was to set the record straight and he is completely frank about his motives. This book, unprecedented in espionage literature, is thus a unique testimony to a very special man. It might seem arrogant for an individual to decide to act against the wishes of his government in the way Cairncross did; but I believe in the integrity of this account by a man of deeply-held convictions. What shines through is that he always followed his conscience. What is equally clear, on the other hand, is the lack of integrity with which the Security Services and Intelligence Establishment behaved, in a way which raises serious questions about their morality and accountability.

All the accusations made against Cairncross crumbled when he finally challenged them. It is now the duty of the Russian government, whose predecessors say he deserved a medal for the help he gave the Russian people during the darkest days of the war, finally to correct the widespread errors about his association with the KGB or to substantiate Modin's latest charges. For their own part, and for the sake of their credibility, MI5 should stop protecting the skeletons of the past at the expense of the truth.

Richard Norton-Taylor, 1997

Editorial Notes

The John Cairncross I knew was a light-hearted and engaging man. When I first met him in Rome in 1984 he was absorbed in a number of projects and spent most of his time writing and translating. However, he always had time for a spirited conversation over a dish of pasta. He seemed to have weathered the storm unleashed by the publication three years earlier of Chapman Pincher's *Their Trade in Treachery* and when, in 1987, Peter Wright's *Spycatcher* appeared, despite the many errors in that book and its predecessor, he refused to speak out. Instead, he quoted to me the Austrian dramatist Grillparzer: 'Why should we seek remembrance of things past? Do they not uninvited haunt us still?'

However, in 1990 he was finally compelled to defend himself publicly when, having just arrived in the south of France, he was labelled as the 'Fifth Man' in a 'Ring of Five' Soviet agents. He disputed this and other charges at length in a statement for the BBC. He then harnessed his considerable analytical powers to studying the origins of the 'Fifth Man' saga. Two essays resulted. The first entitled 'The Fifth Man and other Tall Stories', was followed immediately by 'The Superspy', an article which put forward his theory of the link between these two themes and explained why the attack on him had been motivated by every reason except the search for the truth. Eventually he integrated both essays into this book.

A year later – his refutation ignored – he broke ranks and began to write his autobiography, provisionally entitled *An Agent for the Duration (The Fifth Man that Never Was)*; later he substituted the ironical subtitle '*Memoirs of the Fifth Man*'. He planned his book in three distinct parts: Part I is essentially this book; Part II 'The Road to Disaster' was to consist of his short unpublished history of the Munich

Pact of 1938 entitled *Munich and After* and he later drew upon large sections of it for this book; Part III which would have covered his literary career he whimsically entitled 'He calls himself a writer'. Part III was never written, for by the autumn of 1993 after nearly completing Part I, at the age of eighty-one John suffered a stroke.

During his convalescence, he and I continued to work together on his book and I proceeded to transfer his draft material onto our computer. I also began to look for a publisher. In May 1995, for personal and medical reasons we moved to Britain. John was returning after an absence of more than thirty years and I was entering the country for the first time. Three months later in August he suffered a second stroke, and on 8 October, shortly after we had married, he died. John would now rely on me to ensure that his story would be heard. By that time a provisional plan for publishing his autobiography had been set in train but had not been finalised. A month after his death, I contacted Ronnie Challoner, who agreed to help prepare John's manuscript for publication. Together we were able to finalise the work John had begun in 1991, taking ony one editorial liberty: we implemented John's intentions to open his account with the episode that prompted him to embark upon it – in his 'exposure' as the 'Fifth Man' – by inserting at the beginning his essay 'The Fifth Man and other Tall Stories' under the chapter heading 'The Decoy'. John has chosen to refer to the Soviet Security Services collectively as the KGB (which came into being in 1953) although these were known by various names including NKVD and NKGB during the years of John's association with them. The provisional publishing plan eventually fell through, but John's story soon found an enthusiastic publisher in Random House.

Gayle Cairncross

*

I first met John Cairncross in France through my friend Graham Greene and admired him as a scholar and poet. After he died, Gayle Cairncross invited me to collaborate with her in his memoirs. Together we examined the hand and typewritten versions which John had not had time to incorporate into a final script. Although there was overlapping material and his handwriting was sometimes difficult to interpret, their content shone with clarity. It was evident to me from these and from my personal acquaintance, that John Cairncross had a tenacious streak of independence, a wry Scottish humour and an acute sense of justice – the work was not an apology but a clarification. After cross-checking dates and examining other background notes and papers, we were able to buttress and document the original script with primary source material such as his diary of 1934-45 and his personal letters. After many weeks at the Cairncross cottage in the Welsh Marches, followed later by further meetings and consultations, the Cairncross story was finally ready for publication. Clearly no one looked over his shoulder when writing this extraordinary account – not the KGB and certainly not MI5 or MI6.

R W Challoner

Dedicated to the memory of Graham Greene
1904–1991

Jan. 26. '86.

I have known John Cairncross for forty
three (43) years, we have worked together
during the war, & have been friends ever
since. He is a man of complete honesty
on whose word I would absolutely rely.

Graham Greene

ONE

The Decoy

One sunny September morning in 1990 I was getting the mail from the box outside the gate of my modest rented villa in the South of France when a man walked up and asked me how I felt about the Battle of Kursk. I did not at first register what he was talking about as I had my mind on other things, notably my copy of the *International Herald Tribune* which had just arrived. I finally muttered something non-committal whilst catching my breath at this intrusion. He then followed me uninvited into the garden and introduced himself as Dr Christopher Andrew from Cambridge. Thinking that whatever he was up to would be a rehash of age-old material about my involvement with the KGB*, I decided to put up with his visit, as it would probably get rid of him sooner. And as it was eleven-thirty, I invited him to join my companion Gayle and me for a aperitif of white wine and cassis, a *kir*.

When we were comfortably settled in the shade under the trees he made two requests – one for an interview regarding a book he was writing, and the other for me to take part in a Granada television programme on Soviet defectors. I saw no reason to grant either request and told him so. Andrew then put a number of questions to me, most of which he answered himself. Indeed he did most of the talking. He then advised me to be more forthcoming 'in the interests of history', for, he explained, if I did not tell my story he would be forced to do it for me and he might not get all his facts right. I had no intention of responding to such a crude approach and answered instead that I was waiting for my French residence permit and did not want to draw undue attention to myself. The only substantive contribution made by me in our encounter was three glasses of *kir*.

*The Security Service, known as NKVD (1934-43), NKGB (1943-6) are collectively referred to by JC as the KGB (established 1954).

I

Three months previously, on 19 June, a certain Sheila Kerr had written to me as 'the last surviving member of the Cambridge group' to ask various questions about Donald Maclean on whom she was writing her PhD thesis. She had also mentioned that she was working on a television project about KGB foreign operations and asked if I would care to take part. I had declined firmly but politely. Later in the summer, she appeared at my home with her husband on the flimsy pretext of visiting a friend in the neighbourhood. Though I was busy at the time, I agreed to receive her and spent a morning explaining the position about some Foreign Office documents she had photocopied at the Public Record Office. Mrs Kerr was obviously a qualified researcher but her ideas of Intelligence were somewhat naïve – she seemed to think that KGB moles swapped notes regularly over coffee. She was especially interested in a file containing information on the foreign supply of arms to Spain during the Civil War. I had minuted these files and given them to my superior Donald Maclean with the routine comment that the files contained a 'wealth of valuable information'. She then tried to establish a link between Maclean's post as Head of the American Department and my own work as Deputy Treasury Representative on the Western Union Finance Committee in 1948. She supposed that I had passed on information to Maclean or had told him what I was supplying to the Russians. I could only repeat my response to her in my letter of 9 July 1990: 'Since I only learned of Maclean's activities from the newspapers after his flight, I cannot really help you.'

Soon after Andrew's September visit, I contacted MI5 and warned them of his forthcoming book, thinking that it might also be in their interests to try and keep a lid on the whole affair in order to avoid mutual embarrassment. I had made a full confession to them in 1964 and MI5 had unexpectedly, of their own accord, offered me a qualified grant of immunity from prosecution including the promise of mutual confidentiality. My partial immunity was later to be redefined. I expressed my apprehension of the possible consequences for me, such as the refusal of the French authorities to grant me a residence permit. The MI5 official who, I gathered, was their legal expert, asked me for the name of the author of the book, which I gave him, and he promised to arrange for me to meet a colleague in France with whom I could discuss possible counter-measures. Then, on 25 September, I wrote to my long-time friend Graham Greene in Antibes to ask him to support my application for a residence permit and concluded the letter: 'The hounds of Granada TV are after me as the only survivor of what they so inaccurately call the Cambridge group – although (unlike theirs) my motive [in giving information to the Russians] was to strengthen the Allied cause against the Nazis, and nothing else.'

No one from MI5 contacted me, but a few weeks later I received a telegram from the same Sheila Kerr, who had turned out to be Andrew's assistant, telling me that a Granada TV programme was scheduled for 16 October and would contain references to me which would generate new press interest in my career. She therefore advised me 'to move to a different location for a while' since other journalists were already trying 'to locate your present home'.

I rang up MI5 again and repeated to the same officer my concerns about my French residence permit and the serious financial implications of its possible refusal. The official had forgotten his promise to put me in touch with a colleague and seemed only interested in whether I intended to give my version of events. When I said that, under considerable provocation over many years of inaccurate speculation, I had kept the lowest of profiles and suggested that I should have the right to defend myself against this new onslaught of publicity, he calmly replied that I was still bound by my duty to observe confidentiality; if I was in a difficult position, I had only myself to blame. In other words, our agreement was binding only on one side. I drew the necessary if unpleasant conclusions.

The storm broke on Monday morning, 16 October, when I learned from English neighbours that they had heard on BBC radio that a book by Christopher Andrew and Oleg Gordievsky entitled *KGB: The Inside Story*, serialised the previous day in *The Times*, had named me as the Fifth Man in the Cambridge KGB Ring of Five, four of whom had already been publicly unmasked, to whit Guy Burgess, Donald Maclean, Kim Philby and Anthony Blunt. In addition, I was also accused of being the 'first atom spy'.

I was utterly amazed by these false accusations for (as the public had known since 1981) MI5 never hinted that I had been suspected of being the notorious Fifth Man, neither had I ever been linked with atomic spying. But Andrew's surprise visit had not meant just another raking-up of an old scandal. He had been careful to conceal what he had up his sleeve and to keep me in the dark about the contents of his book which was by then already in the final stages of preparation. Indeed, during his visit he had not mentioned – 'in the interests of history' – a word about the Fifth Man. I was rather to lend credibility to an otherwise abstract account by my appearance on secret camera – for, unbeknown to me, our meeting had been filmed from a van hidden in the vineyard across the way, clips of which were later used at the end of his Granada TV programme.

My canonisation in *The Times* as the egregious villain was eagerly accepted by the English press. At the same time, a crowd of French journalists showed up at my gate to ask me questions about this particularly complex English espionage problem which clearly baffled them as much as it puzzled me – the search for the 'mystery man' who could have enabled the four Cambridge moles to escape punishment. Not having any grasp of the background, the French journalists concentrated on whether I admitted Andrew's charges, and any exchange of information with them was therefore unfruitful. All I could do, in face of the flood of questions, was to deny the accusations of my being the Fifth Man and the first atom spy.

Gayle and I left home for a time to avoid them. This was only partly as a result of the warning telegram sent by Sheila Kerr, my absence was naturally taken as a confession of guilt – and it was even surmised by some newspapers that I had defected to Russia. After we returned from a short exile of dog-sitting in Cotignac, a village ten minutes away, interest subsided somewhat. So when a young M. Herzberg of *Le Monde* telephoned, he caught me by chance – I was awaiting an important personal call. He wanted an interview, and began to ask me questions, but I confined myself to denying that Blunt had ever been my tutor at Cambridge, that I was quite unaware of being the Fifth Man and that I had never been an atom spy. I also tried, in vain, to explain that I was debarred by the British Official Secrets Act from discussing the accusations against me quite as frankly as I would have wished, which he later reported as my being the subject of legal proceedings. Herzberg finally came out with the old gambit that if I refused to talk, journalists would write whatever they fancied, to which I made the equally disingenuous reply that this is exactly what in many cases they had already done. He countered this by saying that anything *The Times* published must by definition be true: a unique testimonial! His subsequent article baldly and inaccurately stated that I had emerged from my silence to give him the interview.

Andrew's book had not yet reached the continental market, and at Saint Antonin du Var in the Provençal countryside I was cut off from the English press. The *International Herald Tribune*, which I received daily by mail, had not yet shown interest in this story. Fortunately, I was sent cuttings on Andrew's work by a host of friends, both in Europe and, what was particularly important, in America, for comments from that quarter were more balanced and detached. But I still needed Andrew's book itself in the preparation of my rejoinder, and this was presented to me in mid-October 1990 by Yves Salomon, the Paris correspondent of *France Soir* in exchange for an interview and for allowing him, as a souvenir, to have his picture taken by photographer Jacques Munch while handing the book over to me.

Andrew had published various studies on Intelligence matters, and had acquired a certain reputation in that field, but *KGB: The Inside Story* was derivative and pedestrian. Therefore, in order to sell his tome of 700 pages, the identification of me as the Fifth Man was placed on the front burner, and a barrage of astute publicity was developed to attract media attention. On the back cover were photographs of the Four Great KGB Moles in their youth, while the newly discovered Fifth Man appeared as a mysterious silhouette, replaced in later editions, I am told, by a photograph of me in an advanced state of decrepitude. I only had to study one solitary passage of roughly ten pages in order to focus on the 'Cairncross legend'. Not content with simply labelling me as the Fifth Man in a ring of 'dedicated Communists', Andrew did everything possible to show that I had been infected with the Red virus at an early point in my life, and dropped broad hints that I had 'probably' been in touch with Communist agents in Paris such as Willi Münzenberg. In the same way, it was assumed that, as soon as I arrived in Cambridge in 1934, I was already a convinced, indeed an 'open' Communist. Supposedly I had attended frequent meetings with Blunt 'at a series of individual weekly tutorials', and had been recruited soon after; and in 1936, when I decided to plump for a Civil Service career, I had done so on KGB instructions to go underground. All this was pure misinformation or wilful fantasy.

Most of these pages drew upon earlier works repeating old errors. The words 'probably' and 'virtually certain' recurred on almost every page when referring to the charges against me and much of the narrative was based on speculation. Although Andrew's material about me was pitifully flimsy, he had his collaborator – KGB defector Oleg Gordievsky with alleged access to the secret KGB archives – to cast his authoritative mantle over the identification of the Fifth Man and provide the sensational ginger. Their acquaintance in 1986, the year following Gordievsky's exfiltration from Moscow, where he had been acting as an undercover SIS source for many years, was providential and the two men soon teamed up; but Andrew must have started work on his KGB book long before that meeting. Curiously, Gordievsky produced no archival evidence or even documentary reference for his identification of me as the Fifth Man. Nor did he provide any description or any information about the Fifth Man's attributes or deeds. He merely named me as being the missing figure.

If Gordievsky had been studiously vague about his sources, his admirers were at pains to fill in the blanks. Thus one of his most ardent supporters, Lord Annan, came particularly to the fore in his unstinting support for Andrew's book, and in his review of the book in *The Times* of 20 October, 1990 he levelled without a shred of proof the monstrous assertion that I had 'betrayed as many major secrets as Philby'. He also repeated Andrew's accusations about the disclosure of atomic secrets without bothering to qualify his charges by inserting a 'probably' or an 'it is almost certain', as had Andrew. He gave his readers to understand that Gordievsky had obtained a flood of information about me during his 'unprecedented access' to the KGB secret archives over a period of twenty-three years, which apparently included, by a special dispensation, his postings abroad. Gordievsky himself gave a slightly different version at the press conference for the book and admitted, to Andrew's evident embarrassment, that he had never seen a file about me. In an interview with Richard Norton-Taylor in the *Guardian* of 20 October 1990, he went further and conceded that he had no documentary evidence about my identification, his assertions being based simply on 'people in the KGB talking quite openly about Cairncross', which is a far cry from pinning the Fifth Man label on me.

After studying the relevant section of the book and the press reviews, I felt that I could put together enough material to counter most of Andrew's charges. It was now time to make some kind of provisional reply to this welter of vilification. I, who was a radical, a libertarian, a pragmatist and a loner, as well as a decidedly straight character, had been stamped as an ideologue, a fanatical Communist, and a KGB recruit almost since my arrival at Cambridge, as well as a close associate of a patrician and partly homosexual group whose political ideals were diametrically opposed to mine. I therefore accepted the BBC's offer for an interview in Paris as they were willing to fly me there and give me a 'forum for my defence'. What tempted me to accept their proposal, in preference to others I had received, was their promise to let me read, or to read themselves, a statement which I had prepared the night before. On my way from the airport to a BBC apartment in Paris where the filming was to take place, I inquired of the BBC man, David Walter, what was to be the context of the proposed interview. He replied that he did not know, but that he had a deadline of 5 o'clock that day, 31 October.

After a lunch of salmon and Sancerre, the BBC gave me useful advice on the presentation of my statement, and made sure that my paper was typed up – all done most competently in the space of an hour and without the least difficulty, except that they were puzzled that I had written of the 'shirt' system at GC&CS Bletchley (a mistype of mine for 'shift'). As against all this, at the last minute as the staff was finishing setting up the camera, it was decided that my statement was 'too long'. I had thus to settle for the interview *tout court*. In preparing this, Walter and I went rapidly over what he would ask me. I raised objections to such obnoxious questions as Was I a traitor? and Did I communicate information to the Russians? because I had come to Paris to defend myself against Andrew's specific charges, refuted in my statement, and not to be put in the dock. I was more than willing to discuss underlying issues such as Chamberlain's appeasement policy towards Hitler in the 1930s, but I felt I was to a certain extent debarred by my obligation to MI5 from discussing some aspects of my case that might perhaps still affect them.

Despite my objections and against their promise that I would be allowed to defend myself, the BBC cast me in the role of the accused. It became obvious to me that Walter was not up to the opportunities offered by the discussion, and was simply following his instructions mechanically. Their 'exclusive interview scoop' seemed to me to be a well-orchestrated operation designed to obtain a 'confession' but the operation was only in part successful, since my responses were highly evasive.

I tried whenever I could to switch the discussion to some of the central questions which most analyses of this affair had so far failed to address. In this I was singularly unsuccessful. Faced with an aggressive type of question, I could only respond by silence: I was still trying to honour my understanding with the British Security Authorities and was thus confining my answers to denying the many inaccuracies. But my reply to the question 'Do you consider yourself a traitor?' was hardly evasive, and was in fact as brutal as the query. I said that, for me, the main traitor in the Allied camp was Chamberlain himself, since he did untold harm to his side. He had, no doubt with the best intentions, betrayed Czechoslovakia and blundered into war over Poland which led to untold loss of life, suffering and wreckage. I also reminded him that a far greater eminence, de Gaulle, had been condemned to death *in absentia* by Pétain who accused him of treason. What I did not say was that, as the word 'treason' is usually taken to mean collusion with a country's enemies, especially if that country is occupied by the foe, and Germany was our main enemy, I never considered myself a traitor to Britain, but a patriot in the struggle against Nazism.

To judge from the disgruntled look on Walter's face, he was not too happy with the tone and manner of my responses. I am sure he was more comfortable with my evasiveness as he had not been prepared for my combative style. But he had a chance to recover his aplomb, as all his questions to me had to be re-taped, for the BBC used only one camera throughout, which they trained exclusively on me. And, indeed, instead of rendering the real atmosphere of this exchange, the interview as broadcast gave the impression that he was in complete control of the talk.

The reason for the 5 o'clock deadline became clear much later when I learned that the interview was part of the general flurry of publicity about the newly discovered Fifth Man and was only an overture to a BBC *Newsnight* programme, featuring a panel of reputable experts, with Andrew as the star performer, beamed by satellite from New York. My own statement was not referred to on the programme and indeed any reference to my 'defence' was avoided. And though Walter later indicated that the statement would be distributed to the press, it eventually found its way to Reuters where it must have gathered quite a lot of dust.

When challenged by Chapman Pincher on that programme, Andrew tried to substantiate his ranking of me but evaded the issue by saying that it was for the KGB to decide on gradings. What he did not say was that the Russians had never given me any ranking whatsoever. In fact, the only *really* juicy item in Andrew's book was the charge that I was 'probably' the first atom spy: 'The earliest intelligence on the Anglo-American decision to build an atomic bomb probably came from John Cairncross.' When that unsubstantiated assertion went unchallenged, he went a step further and claimed that it was virtually certain that I was guilty. The sole reason advanced by him for this sweeping innuendo was that my name appeared on the cover sheet of the minutes of a meeting of the Cabinet Scientific Advisory Committee (SAC) as the Joint Secretary. This body dealt with, among other things, the theoretical analysis of the construction of the atomic bomb. The strange logic of Andrew's accusation was that, if I had access to the information, I must have provided it to the Russians. As a matter of fact, my designation as Joint Secretary on that document's cover sheet was a clerical error, and, as far as I can ascertain, the mistake only occurred once. The confusion was understandable, for I was at the time private secretary to the Chairman of the Committee, Lord Hankey. When, in August, Sheila Kerr had appeared on my doorstep, I had also explained that the secretaries of Hankey's Cabinet Committees had been under the direction of Sir Edward (now Lord) Bridges in the Cabinet Office. This could easily have been confirmed by a call to the Cabinet Office, but no notice was taken of this correction and Andrew brandished a copy of the document bearing the error on the cover sheet*, and urged the cameras to 'freeze-frame' it as proof of my iniquity.

In his Granada television programme about me of 16 October 1990, he had given an even more vigorous display of histrionic energy by waving an unspecified sheet of paper and shouting: 'The formula for the atomic bomb is . . .' as if that formula had been left lying about in the Public Record Office, or, even worse, as if I had somehow laid hands on it in 1941 and delivered it to the KGB!

By attempting to defend myself and, at the same time, protect MI5's position by not revealing too much, I had grossly underestimated the repercussions of the publication of Andrew's book. It seemed also that the 1964 pact of silence with MI5 was dead. Graham Greene, writing from Switzerland, agreed:

* *See facsimile cover sheet overleaf.*

S E C R E T.

S.A.C.(D.P.)(41)4.   COPY NO. 15

30TH JUNE, 1941.

WAR CABINET.

SCIENTIFIC ADVISORY COMMITTEE.

(DEFENCE SERVICES PANEL).

TRANSALANTIC AIR COMMUNICATIONS AND SUPPLY OF
SKILLED PERSONNEL FROM THE UNITED STATES OF AMERICA.

(Reference: S.A.C.(D.P.)(41)4th Mtg. Conclusion 1).

Note by the Secretary.

The attached notes of a Conference held at
55, Whitehall, S.W.1., on the 26th June, 1941, are
circulated for the information of the Panel.

(Signed) D.H.F. RICKETT.

Great George Street, S.W.1.

30TH JUNE, 1941.

DRAFT MINUTES OF A CONFERENCE HELD AT 55, WHITEHALL,
S.W.1, ON THURSDAY, 26TH JUNE, 1941 AT 3 p.m.

PRESENT:-

The Rt. Hon. Lord Hankey,
Chancellor of the Duchy of Lancaster.
(In the Chair).

Sir Edward Appleton.   Sir Edward Mellanby.

Professor R.H. Fowler.   Sir Henry Tizard,
                                        Ministry of Aircraft Production.

Dr. D.R. Pye.   Major A.A. Ross,
Ministry of Aircraft Production.   Ministry of Aircraft Production.

Mr. S.A. Dismore,   Major A.T. Sumner,
Ministry of Aircraft Production.   Ministry of Supply.

Mr. F. Roffey,   Mr. O.V. Guy,
Ministry of Supply.   Ministry of Labour & National
                                        Service.

Mr. F. Brundrett, Admiralty.

Mr. D. H.F. Rickett......................)Joint
Mr. J. Cairncross........................)Secretaries.

You will probably have heard by this time from Colonel Challoner who is a great friend apart from being Consul General in Nice and obviously still attached, however distantly, to Intelligence. He shared my opinion of the whole business and offered to be of any help to you if it was needed in France. He agreed that the security people had broken their promise to you.

After a meeting at the Consulate in Nice, I responded that his friend was very helpful:

. . . however, his recommendation to me to remain silent, though possibly related to, and justified by, the *séjour* [residence] question, has a suspicious convergence with the command of the authorities to be quiet. I am sure your view that he can be trusted is correct, but the issue remains, in the long run, of the line I should take. As you say, I have clearly been let down. The more I learn, the clearer it is.

I decided that if I were to speak out I would have to answer the question of why the British public had thrown itself with such fervour on the palpable absurdities and tissues of old reports and new slanders about me. I began for the first time to study the works of espionage experts and molehunters such as Peter Wright (whose 1987 *Spycatcher* I had never bothered to read), and Chapman Pincher. Eventually, I hacked my way through the confusing issues of the Fifth Man question. But it took me almost a year to build up a picture both of what had really happened in Moscow and of what was believed in London to have happened, which was usually vastly different. In uncovering the ins and outs of this complex affair, I had to turn molehunter myself.

Although the English have a tendency to accept without hesitation views clad in the mantle of authority, there was no mystery that the mood of the public was prepared for spine-tingling revelations about the interlocking questions of KGB penetration and MI5 cover-ups – circumstances which had created hysteria in Britain's Secret Service since 1951 when Burgess and Maclean had slipped out of the country even when at least the latter had been detected. This calamity had been followed, after some twelve years, by the Philby débâcle. But the general sense of outrage over these escapes paled in comparison to the discovery that an even more scandalous spy, Anthony Blunt, had finally been confronted, in 1964, and then not only given immunity but also allowed to continue undisturbed in his post as Surveyor of the Queen's Pictures until 1979. It was hardly surprising that the man in the street began to suspect that all sorts of vital secrets were being kept from him, and Andrew's book hit this particular nerve.

In 1965, Peter Wright had told me (without revealing his source) that it was the KGB defector Anatoli Golitsyn, who went over to the Americans in 1961, who had brought the idea of the Ring of Five for the first time to the West. Ironically, Gordievsky and Golitsyn were in the same boat: we now know that Golitsyn did not have access to inside information and was therefore misleading on a number of points. For example, he believed that all the members of the Ring of Five had been boys together in their schooldays, and continued their cooperation at Cambridge, and that each was aware of the other's activities. He did not however know the names of its members, except those of Burgess and Maclean who had defected long ago, though he apparently provided details on Philby. Nor did he know any of the members' codenames, nor did he have any idea who the missing figure was. Wright admitted to me that the mystery of the missing agent puzzled him, but according to *Spycatcher* he later became convinced that it was Alister Watson, an atomic scientist. The matter was never thoroughly followed up by MI5 as they were busy with a very controversial in-house drama – the problem of Russian penetration by a Superspy which had been going on for around twenty years. But when Blunt was unmasked by Andrew Boyle, there was a leakage, and a nationwide search developed for the last missing link in British Intelligence who, it was believed, had enabled the four Cambridge moles to function so successfully.

In 1988, two years before Andrew published his book, both Blunt and Philby had stated that the so-called Cambridge ring had only four members. Indeed, Blunt, as part of his confession in 1964, confirmed to Peter Wright (as reported in *Spycatcher*) that the ring 'was only ever a Ring of Four: himself, Burgess, Philby and Maclean, with other recruits like Long and Cairncross existing independently of the central Ring members'. The fact that a group of five agents (recruited through the same channel) had all studied at Cambridge was pure coincidence, and could not be taken to imply that they operated jointly.

Blunt's version was subsequently confirmed by Philby when, just before his death, he was interviewed in Moscow by Phillip Knightley in

January 1988. In summing up Philby's view, Knightley stated: 'There was no Cambridge ring, no Cambridge Comintern cell . . . The whole hunt for the Fifth Man has been a waste of time. If there was no Comintern cell, then why should there be a Fifth Man?' Philby agreed, and added: 'We were recruited individually, and we operated individually. Burgess was the only one who knew all the others, and he maintained the links with all of us.' My own limited experience completely confirms this assertion. And so, if I was not a member of a ring and was ignorant of the existence of the other moles, I do not qualify as the fifth, or even as the twenty-fifth man.

The fall of the Berlin Wall in November 1989 and the collapse of Communism in the Soviet Union (and of a great many other seemingly solid structures) opened up new and important sources of information which would show up the wild errors of Gordievsky and risk putting him back in the cold. The key man in the story was Yuri Modin, my last KGB controller, who still survives in Moscow, hale and hearty despite his advanced age. The former KGB Colonel had stated in a mid-September article in the Soviet magazine *Sovershenno Sekretno* (*Top Secret*) that the Cambridge spies 'were not a team of agents or a Communist Party cell. They all worked independently.'

I was in my garden on 21 September, 1991 when, as usual without prior notice, two people from the *Mail on Sunday* appeared – reporter Fiona Barton and photographer David O'Neill. Since the paper had been particularly active in trying to extract information from Modin, I was interested in hearing what they could tell me. Ms Barton relayed the latest information and asked for my comments. I repeated what I had conjectured after Andrew's book had appeared and what I had then drafted for the BBC in Paris, but which had not been broadcast: that I had been given star billing by the KGB solely because of my contribution to the Russians' victory at Kursk. I emphasised that on that occasion, as always, I had operated independently on my own initiative and not as part of a ring; and that my transmission of ENIGMA Intelligence, while irregular, had not involved the betrayal of any specifically British information. By this approach I hoped to put the newspaper in a position to destroy the inaccurate picture of the Fifth Man which had been adopted in Britain, and thus dispel a major source of confusion in Intelligence analysis.

I was therefore taken by surprise when the *Mail on Sunday* of 22 September went to town in the worst tradition of the yellow press with a 'world exclusive' headline of 'Yes, I'm the Fifth Man'. It declared triumphantly that it had now proven me to be the Fifth Man, after I had denied it, and pilloried me as the mole who had successfully avoided detection but was now convicted of treason. Ms Barton had persuaded me to let her photographer take a picture of me, since 'the other ones were so bad', and this hideous likeness with the caption 'The face of a traitor', was published in the early edition. In later editions it was replaced by a reasonable photograph of me with two of my dogs. I have had few such unpleasant encounters with the press. The *Mail on Sunday*, when offered an opportunity to clarify the Fifth Man issue was only interested in extracting the last ounce of scandal from the affair. The historical situation – the survival of Britain as an independent power, and even my attitude about the importance of that issue and the small part I played in it – took second place. This was precisely the kind of contretemps which I had been anxious to avoid and which I might well have escaped had MI5 been willing, as previously promised, to talk to me and advise me. My attempts to try to enlighten the popular press had shown a complete absence of the cunning usually regarded as an essential ingredient of the spy's make-up. I wrote to the *Mail on Sunday* objecting to their article and I got a reply from Fiona Barton saying that she was 'very grateful for your courtesy and cooperation . . . I felt, as you did, that it was time the myths and innuendoes were laid to rest . . .'

Modin's statement of September was confirmed and expanded in an interview with Tom Bower in the *Sunday Telegraph* of 17 November, 1991. Modin explained what was behind Golitsyn's report of a Ring of Five in 1943 and cleared up the mystery. He had been working as head of the British Empire section of the KGB Centre in Moscow when the flow of top secret information was such that a priority system had to be devised in order to make it possible to cope with the material. The task of selecting the section's key agents had fallen to him, and the five men finally chosen – five being a favourite Russian number – were known as the *Pyatchorka* or group of five and not a ring, since they had all operated individually. I was the third on this alphabetical list, sandwiched between Burgess and Blunt and Maclean and Philby. My inclusion was due to the enormous importance attached by the Russians to the secret ENIGMA information on German operations on the Russian front which I had supplied. Here at last was the origin of the Ring of Five concept. My own interpretation, at which I had arrived independently, coincided with Modin's information: but what he did not say was that I probably was not kept on the priority list after I had left Bletchley in 1943, when the flow of vital military intelligence from me had dried up.

By entering the Fifth Man scene in 1990, Andrew and Gordievsky had been a year too early to be in possession of the full facts, which disposed of the idea of a Cambridge ring larger than four. As Gordievsky had claimed unparalleled access to the KGB's most secret archives he was presumed to be in a position to know the truth, but in reality he knew almost nothing relevant to these issues. Any corridor gossip he had heard about me was more likely connected to my inclusion on the *Pyatchorka* list of 1943, and was unrelated to the Fifth Man story as it developed in the West: but as forty years had elapsed since the genesis of the list, and he had only worked in its archives after 1981, he had confused the two. Thus, because 'five-man rings' are a Russian tradition, it had been surmised that a fifth Cambridge mole of the same metal as Burgess, Maclean, Blunt and Philby was still unknown to the public.

More recent disclosures from Moscow and London shed additional light on the confusing Fifth Man question. According to information released from the KGB's files by Oleg Tsarev and John Costello, and reproduced in their book *Deadly Illusions*, I was the sixth and not the fifth man. Chronologically speaking (in order of their recruitment) the Fifth Man (after Blunt, Burgess, Philby and Maclean) had been the American Michael Straight, who figured prominently in the English side of the story only when he had denounced Blunt in 1964.

If a distinction has to be made between the joint authors of *KGB: The Inside Story*, I would certainly regard Andrew as the moving spirit, but I suspect that British Intelligence was not an insignificant factor behind this imbroglio. This charge is difficult to prove, but the supporting circumstantial evidence is very strong. For example, the well-known author on Intelligence matters, James Rusbridger, wrote that Gordievsky's original tale: 'as permitted by MI6 was quite modest, but has perhaps fallen under Dr Andrew's influence with the result that it has been extensively hyped up.' Phillip Knightley also heavily discounted Gordievsky's contribution to the analysis of the KGB's activities and pointed out in an article for the *Spectator* of 3 November, 1990 that: 'in a sense Gordievsky is still working for SIS, and this book was submitted for official approval before it was published.' His entry into current polemics is in line with his visit to Eton, where he was chaperoned by a former head of the Foreign Office. And Andrew himself had drawn substantially on inside sources in composing his earlier works on British Intelligence. He also must have known perfectly well that I could not come to Britain to defend myself in the courts. MI5 could hardly be expected to come out in my defence, but by remaining silent had in effect condoned the book even though, in the view of the distinguished historian Sir Michael Howard, 'there are in it a great many things which the agency knows are not true.'

In reviewing the various press stories, I had noted an eloquent difference between those journalists who had swallowed the Andrew version of events uncritically and those who had pointed out some of its blatant weaknesses. A most revealing comment on Andrew's flawed scholarship had been made by CIA officials as reported by Francis Wheen in the *Independent on Sunday* of 14 November, 1990. At an interview at the CIA Headquarters at Langley, says Wheen, Gordievsky 'seemed embarrassed by all the hype surrounding the book'. This admission was in complete contradiction to the claim made on his behalf in the book's unsigned Introduction which stated:

> Gordievsky had long had a deep interest in KGB history as well as in its current operations. In 1980 he had been responsible for preparing the sections of a highly classified in-house history of the First Chief Directorate, dealing with KGB operations in Britain, Ireland, Scandinavia, and Australia.

According to Wheen, when asked 'why there were so many gaps – and errors – in the book, Gordievsky impressed his CIA hosts by honestly admitting that he didn't know. He gave the impression that his personal story was not particularly glamorous and had perhaps been inflated in a public relations exercise beyond his control.' It may be suggested that this is only one man's report, but it is consistent with the fact that there is not a single statement about me in Andrew's book which is both original and substantiated. At the same press conference mentioned earlier Gordievsky also alleged that another KGB colleague, Dmitri Svetanko, had reported that I had supplied 'literally tons' of documents to the KGB. I find it difficult to imagine how I transported them under my jacket unless it was in the car the Russians are supposed to have given me at a time when I did not drive and when wartime petrol was severely rationed.

On 4 October, 1992 an article appeared in the *Washington Post* making fresh revelations, based on documents made available by the KGB, about the depth and extent of atomic espionage by the Russians. In a spirit of openness, several espionage files had been released in Moscow and the only point which needs to be quoted here is that on 25 September, 1942 a report had been sent to the KGB's Moscow Centre by Anatoli Gorsky of the London Rezidentura. This stated that, at a meeting of the SAC held nine days earlier, British scientists had expressed confidence that a uranium bomb could be produced within two years. The source of this information was given as Donald Maclean's personal file, which showed that he had been responsible for the leak which Andrew had been so keen to attribute to me. I might add that on the BBC *Newsnight* programme of 31 October, 1990 on the Fifth Man, Robert Cecil, formerly of the Foreign Office and author of an authoritative biography of Maclean, asserted that the only confidential information divulged at the SAC meetings up to the end of my stint with Lord Hankey, was that work on the atomic bomb was to be transferred to America; but by the time they had taken the decision to do so I had been posted to Bletchley.

It was always refreshing to turn to the balanced and searching analysis made by American reviewers and experts. In a review for the *Wall Street Journal* of 13 December, 1990 entitled 'Not the Inside Story', Tennent H. Bagley, a former Deputy Chief of the CIA's Soviet Division, was severe in his criticism of *KGB: The Inside Story*. He wrote that Andrew's material was overfamiliar to informed readers and added that the writer had 'given Gordievsky credit for more than fifty pieces of information that were either self-evident or reported long ago'. More importantly, Andrew's own contribution was flawed: 'He has taken shortcuts in the historian's disciplines that diminish the book's authority. He often leans on a single source, while overlooking more reliable ones, and by trusting earlier writers who got their information second-hand, he has perpetuated mistakes that any knowledgeable reader will spot.'

Bagley is equally critical of Andrew's co-author:

> Gordievsky's contribution offers nothing (repeat nothing) original. What he gives us instead are trivial tidbits and inside gossip, which we find sprinkled like tinseled flakes over a Christmas package, to make Andrew's compendium of old cases look more shiny-new and inside-authoritative than it really is. We learn of no previously unknown spies ... Although co-signed by Gordievsky, the book is full of statements that no recent KGB professional would be expected to make or endorse.

He also comments that 'the book is studded with avoidable errors', and that these 'are given the stamp of Gordievsky's authority'.

But Andrew was given his worst beating by Arthur Schlesinger Jr. In an article in the *Atlantic Monthly* of March 1991, Schlesinger described the book as 'exasperating' and contributing nothing new. Writing in the same vein as Bagley, he pointed out that it is 'mainly a rehash of familiar names and events, and is largely derived from secondary sources ... One is struck by Andrew's credulity. He seems to swallow as gospel everything that Gordievsky and other ex-Communists say.' Schlesinger went even further when he said that the book 'has such shoddy aspects that one is inclined to retract one's regard for Andrew's earlier works'.

The section of the book which aroused Schlesinger's indignation (and which had been based only on a KGB officer's lecture to colleagues) was the smear on Harry Hopkins, Roosevelt's special envoy, as 'an unwitting Soviet agent'. Andrew later admitted that Hopkins was a sincere patriot whose firm determination to help defeat Hitler led him to emphasise the need to give Russia the maximum aid. But Hopkins was not the only American whom Andrew and his collaborator denounced as a controlled Soviet agent. The same charge was made against Harry Dexter White of the State Department. On such tricks, Schlesinger commented, 'Gordievsky does not claim to have seen files on NKVD operations in the United States. Instead, Andrew provides a potted account of Soviet espionage in America drawn from published and sometimes dubious sources, and interspersed with Gordievsky's recollections of KGB corridor gossip. No wonder,' concludes Schlesinger, that 'the book is spiced with sensational stories about dead men. One trusts that the six-figure advance will make up for the damage done to the author's reputation and credibility.'

Having already done everything within my power to assist the Security Service in fulfilment of my agreement with Arthur Martin and Peter Wright of MI5 in 1964, I can hardly be blamed for feeling dismayed by the fact that my actions had been misrepresented and the public misled about my motives. But it had gradually dawned on me that the naming of me as the Fifth Man might be a concerted campaign in an attempt to close the chapter on any further discussion of Soviet penetration of the Security Service. My role had been simply that of a fall guy – the decoy!

When the storm broke over me in the autumn of 1990 I had nearly completed writing a book, *Munich and After,* about the crisis of September 1938 and Chamberlain's policy of appeasement amounting to surrender, which I had planned to publish in America under the pseudonym David Jardine. After learning of Andrew's wild charges against me I decided to come into the open and also tell the story of my relations with the KGB. The two subjects are closely linked, as my early familiarity with European countries and languages was largely responsible for my concern, at a very early stage, with the Nazi menace of Germany and the deadly danger it presented to Britain and its Allies. Graham Greene wrote encouragingly:

> I think you should perhaps keep in the background until your right of *séjour* is established. Then I think you should come again, if you wish, out of the shadows and I think a book is an excellent idea.
>
> I was amused by the press cuttings and the angry exchanges between the various authors of books about the Secret Service who have had no experience of the Service themselves.
>
> PS. I wonder when the hacks will begin to look for a sixth man!

It may seem strange that a confessed Soviet agent should find fault with MI5 for its incompetence in not distinguishing between my actions, which were pro-Allied, and the four Cambridge moles, who were pro-Communist and ideologist. I am, in fact, the last man to enthuse about Communist doctrine. Even so, the Security Service never bothered to examine me about my beliefs and motives, merely assuming that I had always been a dedicated Communist. The fact is, I had cut off all connection with the Communist Party long before I went down from Cambridge in June 1936, and I had never joined the Party. My desire was to contribute to the resistance to Nazi aggression. This had been my main concern and my only involvement with the political scene up to and including my Cambridge days: without an understanding of this, my later decisions would be inexplicable.

I can undoubtedly be accused of recklessness, arrogance and naiveté for finally deciding, in the light of Britain's wartime plight, to deliver secret ENIGMA intelligence to the Russians. But there is no way this can be called treason. I am therefore, at my ripe old age, still naïve enough to believe that this account of my life – warts and all – will ring true.

TWO

Red Hair is Dangerous

When I was thirteen, an old man in the village of Lesmahagow where I was born in 1913, prophesied a not exactly bright future for me. He had the reputation of being the local sage, and while tending his tomatoes in his hothouse, mellowed by a draught of whisky, he made the singular prophecy that I would get into some serious scrapes in life, but would emerge safely in the end. I was not given to introspection as a child: mine was an open and exuberant nature, impatient of constraint, even rebellious, and not at all canny or down-to-earth as Scots are often pictured. Perhaps one could say that the Celtic side of the Scots character was most marked in me: emotional, poetic, imaginative and impractical. P.G. Wodehouse sums up my personality acutely: 'Nature,' he says, 'made the grave mistake of creating redheads who are always so impulsive and quick on the trigger.' He could have added that they have little hesitation in standing up for their opinions regardless of the sensitivity of their less ardent fellow men and women. These red-headed genes, then, were decisive in shaping body and soul. The spontaneity and fervour with which I expressed my feelings were usually met with surprise or silence and I would often feel enraged when I sensed that I was being patronised by adults. Thus I failed to give the old man's prediction much attention, but I never forgot his words, which not only pointed to a troubled future but also showed that I was already at odds with Scottish orthodoxy.

Lesmahagow is a small village 23 miles from Glasgow on the main road leading south to England, and its history probably goes back to the founding of a church, the *ecclesia* of St Machutus, in the twelfth century. With the discovery and exploitation of coal in the nearby village of Coalburn, the emphasis changed somewhat from fruit growing, for which the Clyde valley has always been famous, but we remained apart from the grime of the coalpits. The countryside began just above our house, and I used to accompany one of my brothers when he helped to milk the cows on the nearest farm. It has now become a commuters' centre and an outpost of Glasgow's metropolis, but back then we were a small, self-contained rural community – simple, stable and calm in every aspect. Cars were the privilege of the rich or the professional. I first heard the miraculous sounds of radio when I was five, and I was fourteen when electricity replaced gas at home. I have been conveniently defined, by those writers who project the English social structure on to Scotland, as of working-class origin (a facile Communist stereotype) and as a rebel against social injustice. In fact, my parents were sturdy middle-class, and though we were not high up the ladder, my father was proud of his relative eminence. With his partner, he ran the local ironmonger's store.

Most people think of the Clyde valley as a hotbed of labour agitation and it is sometimes referred to as Red Clydeside. Naturally, there was a political cleavage between the middle-class villagers and the miners. The former, like my father, were staunch Conservatives, while the miners voted Labour, and at elections this basic antagonism would emerge. Neither party had much ambition to change the social system and even at the height of the General Strike in 1926 there was no violence in our village, only a march of the workers to the Town Hall to demand the reversal of a decision to suspend relief payments to the strikers. After the Town Clerk had addressed the demonstrators and agreed to this concession (which, though he did not say it, was only temporary), the crowd dispersed peacefully. The coalmines have long been closed and this source of tension is now a thing of the past.

It is probably not surprising that most of my early recollections are of my mother, who provided a special harmony in my early home life. She started life as an elementary schoolteacher, and her children's success in their studies was sometimes put down to her coaching, but her vast household duties left her scant time for watching over our studies. Looking back, I find it amazing that she could devote so much attention to one child when there were seven others to be cherished, for I was the youngest of eight: four boys and four girls. Our needs were simple – food and basic clothing – but even there economy was practised. We used to banter her when, if we left something in the centre dish, she would say with light-hearted resignation, 'Well, I'll just need to take it myself.' But there was never much time left for frivolous extras in such a large family where there was a host of things to be seen to by the lady of the house. Even with the aid of a live-in maid, which was then available and affordable, she usually had her hands full with chores. One fine day, my brothers and sisters joyfully ran our now useless pram to its end in the garden behind the house and I realised happily that I was to be the last arrival in the family.

I had no difficulty in accepting the authority of my father or in complying with his wishes for there was always friendly contact between children and parents even if there was never a strong feeling of intimacy in our relationship. What was special about the atmosphere of my home life, which in a way makes up for all its conventionality, was the deep respect for learning which inspired us all. Early on I turned to the world of reading, and especially literature, as my main source of excitement and inner development. I had even then a keen interest in the exotic and my first book, purchased at the age of six, was an illustrated selection from the *Arabian Nights Entertainments*. It cost sixpence, and I had only fourpence, but a generous bystander chipped in with the missing twopence and I was able to depart in triumph with my prize. It was to become my favourite reading as soon as a more complete copy was added to our library at home.

I was imbued with a roving spirit and, when I had time on my hands, I would take off on my own. I once, still at a very young age, surprised a shopkeeper at the opposite end of the village when I called on him unaccompanied and tried in vain to buy some sweets. I nevertheless soon settled down, took full advantage of my opportunities and concentrated on what could be learned at school. The fact of speaking a patois from childhood, especially one with such rich traces of, for example, French and Scandinavian in its vocabulary, reduced for me any feeling of constraint in speaking a foreign tongue. I remember my mother calling me a 'footer' (meaning to potter about and derived from the French *foutre*) when she was annoyed with me, unaware of the (greatly weakened) sexual implications of the word. And, when learning Swedish, I recognised quite a few terms which were embedded in the dialect. For example, 'speir' (*spörja* in Swedish) means to ask, and 'flit', (*flytta*) means to move house. I also had a facility for mimicry, a good ear for music and an excellent verbal memory, which made languages the natural choice, so I was able to seek exoticism nearer home in French and German literature. And, since education was the highest priority, we were allowed to follow whichever paths our natural talent or the educational system permitted. Where the school did not supply all our wants, we had recourse to outside teachers. My parents even insisted on my having piano lessons, possibly because they knew that the teacher, an elderly woman who lived down the hill, was in need of the money. I would never have pressed for this and in fact was not really keen, but such opportunities were not to be ignored. Mine was a studious youth.

My family were regular churchgoers without being 'holier than thou'. I was never a natural believer, but I attended divine service regularly out of respect for my parents. I always enjoyed the resounding cadences of the Authorised Version which, with Shakespeare, has been for me, as for so many English speakers, the foundation of my feeling for the English language. I later developed from these early days an intense interest in the exegesis of New Testament accounts of Christ's crucifixion, which was not given a historical explanation in the gospel versions. Presbyterian fervour showed itself indirectly in my argumentative temperament, which sometimes took on a Talmudic intensity and, though this tendency has been softened by the passage of time, the search for doctrinal clarity is deeply rooted in Calvinists. I remember a large framed picture in our dining-room which showed a congregation deserting the established church as a protest against its unacceptable doctrines. This divergence was mirrored in our small village, where there were no fewer than three different Presbyterian churches.

I felt at odds early on with the inhibitions of a Calvinist society, and my aspirations were generally out of line with standard Scottish patterns. Strengthened by the pagan tradition which in Scotland flows just below the surface, I developed strong reservations about the prevailing Puritan morality. This later led me to cultivate an active interest in the history of sexual attitudes. I was influenced by Molière's free-thinking views expressed in *Tartuffe* and *L'Ecole des femmes* (a radical plea for women's emancipation). A most useful source on sexual mores from the French Renaissance was Pierre de Bourdeille Brantôme's *Lives of Gallant Ladies* – a work which in the contemporary context is decidedly pro-women. Other subjects which greatly interested me were the history of the family, birth control and demography.

Even if I did look elsewhere for spice and colour, I always supported and admired such native virtues as straightforwardness, decency, honesty and independence. The Scots are often dismissed as a difficult and unsophisticated race, lacking in the social graces, but it is also true that they are no great respecters of persons, unlike the English who always seem to have an eye cocked at their neighbours or colleagues; and it is not for nothing that the motto of Aberdeen's Marishal College is: 'They say. What say they? Let them say.' Ideally, one should have a range of virtues embracing contradictory or mutually exclusive qualities, but the world is not made to accommodate such catholicity.

My life outside the home began at the regulation age of five, when I started going to the village school. The infants' section was separate, and lay across the River Nethan, a tributary of the Clyde, in what was the poorer section of the village, called Turfholm. In class, we still used sheets of slate to write on with squeaky chalk pencils, and these were only replaced by paper some years later. My schooldays were industrious and carefree. An egalitarian spirit prevailed within the school and classes were coeducational, which was a great blessing, and I developed an early appreciation of the qualities of the opposite sex. Most of the teachers, at least in the junior classes, were women. It was a highly-regarded profession, but this esteem was in part due to the fact that they could take a long holiday during the summer and still draw their salary: 'Aye the pay gain' on,' as the local saying was. One teacher even insisted that we boys should also learn sewing, and this is a task I still do reasonably well today. Later, at Cambridge, I was shocked at the exclusion of women in academia.

Education in Scotland was not only excellent, but also virtually free, and anyone with a desire to get ahead could profit from it, thanks to numerous scholarships. This explains why five of our family of eight took university degrees (and three of the boys later became professors). The zeal for upward mobility was for greater prestige rather than financial reward, and we had plenty of examples of local success stories, such as Alexander Lindsay, at one time the Master of Balliol College, Oxford, and Dr Glover, a famous psychoanalyst who once fished out a coloured ball to reassure me on my first train journey when I had become startled by sudden jolts. Both came from the local schoolmaster's house before my time. In my own generation, my brother Sir Alec Cairncross became Economic Adviser to the British

Government before he retired, like so many top civil servants, to the mastership of an Oxbridge college, in his case St Peter's.

As my father married late, by the time I was born he was old enough to be my grandfather. This, coupled with a Scots restraint, made for a lack of intimacy between us. My retentive memory was visible early on and my successes in exams were the occasion of our most friendly contacts. He was proud of my triumphs and generous in his appreciation of them, and the ten shilling note which he gave me when he learned of my first major coup – I came fifth (a year ahead of time) in the open scholarship exam for Glasgow University – represented immense wealth to me. My father had not received much formal schooling, but had an inborn talent for figures and was hence always in demand as an unofficial adviser on tax and inheritance problems. With the right training, he would have made an admirable chartered accountant and my brother Alec certainly inherited his actuarial brilliance. My trouble was that, being the youngest, I never got to know him well and had little knowledge of his many virtues which I would have appreciated had I been in closer contact with him. I was probably not respectful enough of his rugged honesty and frankness, and sometimes I felt slightly irritated by his tendency to quote proverbs. Nevertheless, he had drive and zest and was even regarded by his business partner as a rather rash operator. He was certainly an innovator and he made it a practice, long before such a gesture was common, to grant a joiner a ten per cent discount if he could show his trade union card. He had, I suspect, a considerable capacity for enjoying life, though he was careful not to manifest it too publicly, and a healthy sex drive, as his eight children testified. I like to think that I, too, take after him in more ways than one.

My brother Alec and I, the last two members of the family, were brought up together and shared the same bedroom and in many respects we were alike. We were both critical of any obviously orthodox proposition, however widely accepted; egalitarian and impatient of pretence and dogmatism. In my early years I lived in Alec's shadow, for he was not only older, but had the added authority of a clear and self-assured approach to most questions. His personality was marked by originality in a conservative mould and he had a strikingly positive nature; he would always make up his mind on issues and would strive for a reasonable and expedient solution to problems. I was more impulsive and temperamental, more open to conflict and to conflicting views. My motto might have been: 'In my house there are many mansions.' When I was as young as eight, the headmaster of the local school, who happened to be looking in at the classroom, remarked dismissively that I was not a patch on my brother. As I was always head of the class, I remained speechless before his authority; even high standards and accomplishments do not exempt one from observing rules of appearance, and with my non-conformist nature I would never learn to observe these rules. My brother and I parted company when, at the age of nineteen, I went off to Paris for two years, but we met again when I went up to Cambridge, since his last year there coincided with my first. We always got on together, but there can be no doubt that, from the day I resigned from the Civil Service in 1952, relations between us were complicated by my spy story which I kept secret, the motives behind which I never explained to him. Thus he would later have some considerable trouble in understanding my joy at leaving England to live in Italy, which was a liberation for me in every way. As he has always felt at home in England, my decision struck him as quite irresponsible.

After village school, I went on to the Academy, or high school, at Hamilton, where I spent two years. This was an uneventful time and I remember little except for a misguided attempt to remodel the Academy along the lines of an English public school, with a system of prefects or class leaders, of whom I was appointed one. I looked so young and so inexperienced at the time that my presence at a prefects' meeting was challenged by a master as being unjustified. Fortunately the new system soon died a natural death, as anyone could easily have predicted. Our basically egalitarian pattern of society rejected the idea of putting someone in charge, especially as we were a perfectly orderly and responsible group. This was my first encounter with English upper-class values, and it was to initiate a long series of clashes between their principles and my own character.

Because I had already won a scholarship, I skipped a year at Hamilton and was impatient to get ahead with my education. This led me, at the age of seventeen, to Glasgow University, where I lived in digs with my brother and an agreeable friend, Ian Smith, returning home at weekends and during the holidays. I was still so unworldly that I bungled an approach by an utterly charming shopgirl who asked me if I 'ever went out'. On a more familiar level, I continued to study the history of Christianity, with articles from *The Hibbert* on whether Christ was crucified or, as it reads alliteratively in the Bible, was 'hanged on a tree'. I also had my first contact with organised politics and I got caught up in the recently-founded movement, then in the ascendant, of Scottish Nationalism. I felt, and still feel, that we in Scotland have a right to a national identity, as we are a country with a separate legal system, a different established church and a separate dialect, quite apart from having a Celtic language still extant in the Highlands. We are an integral part of Great Britain, and not a province annexed by England, whose citizens are often referred to as English – as Sir Alexander Fleming, the Scottish-born and educated discoverer of penicillin, is usually described.

At Glasgow University I continued with my French and German studies, and also took Economics as an extra subject in my first year. This was, after all, the university of Adam Smith, who was regarded as the founder of the discipline. The honours degree course in Modern Languages covered five years and provided, in its third year, for a year at a French Lycée to be followed by a further two years back at Glasgow. I had hoped to be sent to Paris but was in fact offered a post as assistant English teacher at Clermont-Ferrand, a pleasant but unexciting city in the Auvergne in the heart of France. But my parents generously offered to let me spend that year in Paris, where I would attend courses at the famous Sorbonne.

My first extensive excursion outside Scotland was in the summer of 1932 when I set out for Paris. I cycled across to Hull where I took a steamer to Ostend and cycled via Brussels through Belgium to Cologne. I continued on to Passau where I took a boat down the Danube to Vienna and I spent a week in a Youth Hostel. Living there was cheap – it had to be for my purse. Foreign visitors were bathed in a romantic haze of waltz music, operetta and brilliant cabaret. The glory of the powerful Habsburg Empire had largely departed but there was still the cluster of superb baroque churches and palaces, a marvellous art museum and the splendid Opera House where I could buy a standing room ticket for a nominal sum. I enjoyed Wagner's *Das Rheingold* and some delicious Mozart. The people were full of fire and enthusiasm for music, not to mention 'women and wine', but the city was also full of beggars, and half the people I met were unemployed. It was clear that the economic crisis had hit the Austrian people very hard. The country was suffering from violent hostility between the Social Democrats and the governing party of Christian Democrats under Dr Dollfuss; and the large Jewish community would offer a natural target for the Nazis who were becoming more and more powerful.

From Vienna I took the train to Paris and rented cheap rooms in the Latin Quarter. My first lodgings in the old Rue de la Bucherie looked out over Notre Dame and were within walking distance of the Sorbonne. Later I moved to rooms near the Pantheon, almost across the road from the students' usual reading library, the Mont Sainte Geneviève. At mealtimes I invariably ate at the students' club or in cheap restaurants in the district. This would not be possible now, because all those little cafés have given way to smart tea-rooms and, as recently as 1984, after I had given a short address on Thai history to a circle of Asian specialists, we had the last meal in one of the few surviving restaurants behind the Sorbonne. I had never experienced wine in Scotland, apart from at an occasional celebration, but a small carafe was included in the fixed price meal in Paris, so I started drinking wine regularly and developed a taste for it. That was, alas, to be my only vice. I was naturally expected on my arrival in Cambridge to have indulged in a round of *amours* in Paris, and I was later to be guilty of shameless bluff or feigned discretion when talking of my Paris days. The sad fact is that I had no sex life when living there, largely because I had nowhere to engage in it, for taking a girl back to my lodgings was strictly forbidden. As a waggish friend of mine suggested: 'No sex please, we're French.' I remember being struck by what seemed to me the stereotype of 'gay Paree', with such shows as the Folies Bergères, and its greater openness about sex, and the fact that most of the men I knew seemed to have mistresses. At the same time, paradoxically, relations with women were governed by a very strict Victorian code.

Most of my colleagues in class were *Action Française*, a reactionary monarchist movement which I found anachronistic. They were anticlerical and authoritarian and reflected the general scepticism and distrust of the corrupt parliamentary system which later provoked riots by the right-wing. Otherwise I remained unaware of France's economic problems largely because, being an agricultural country, people did not suffer from the squalor and unemployment of many other European countries. Their backward social facilities and iniquitous taxation (the French simply refused to pay their taxes) would create tensions which would surface only later under the Popular Front. There was a French Communist party, but it seemed isolated from the rest of the Left.

I spent this first year in Paris wrapped in a kind of academic cocoon, taking little interest in politics, but I appreciated French sophistication and the apparent absence of class snobbery. I concentrated with scholarly enthusiasm on the cultural life of the city and sought to acquire the French talent for clear and orderly exposition. I gave myself up to cultivating French literature over a broad spectrum of periods and works, especially Baudelaire, one of the greatest poetic geniuses in European history. Nietzsche says that French life and culture are ideal for the process of *déniaisement*, which means at bottom waking the mind up to the complexities and less rosy sides of life, and I can only agree heartily for, if anyone needed this treatment, it was me. The brilliant French films of the period (1932–1934), such as *Topaze* with Louis Jouvet, were unforgettable. That film now seems a trifle crude, but in fact there was nothing easier for an immature young soul to absorb than unmitigated and highly simplified cynicism. And there was the slight perfume of decay in the bittersweet lyrics of songs such as '*Je ne crois plus au Père Noël*', or '*Aimons-nous ce soir sans songer . . .*', and who could blame the French after the ghastly bloodletting of the First World War?

The masterpieces of French literature also represented a fundamental enrichment of my culture and knowledge, although their impact was sometimes less immediate. The great French classics, including the exquisite music and simplicity of Racine's dramatic verse, the fables of La Fontaine and Molière's plays in particular, were far more than a source of aesthetic pleasure. The great comic writer Molière has always been an inspiration to me, and I was thinking of him specifically when I wrote the lines:

Laughter's hand alone can bind
The ligaments of heart and mind.

His is indeed a rich and varied oeuvre. He was a scourge of affectation, pedantry and narrow asceticism, and I have always admired him as the champion of the liberation of women, especially as regards the choice of mate. I still regard his *Don Juan* as an unforgettable and immortal masterpiece, which shows just how dubious are the orthodox certitudes and canons of this world. But I also found stimulus in less orthodox works, such as André Gide's *Nourritures Terrestres*, which describes his liberation from the shackles of a severe Protestant asceticism which had prevented him from enjoying life in the round, and Georges Duhamel's fine novels *Deux Hommes* and *Confession de Minuit*, and even the risqué literature of Pierre Louÿs.

All these new-found facets of culture, not to mention the influence of French life, left me with a much more sophisticated appreciation of not only poetry, but also of the complexity and the ironies of life. Perhaps what appear to be the firm foundations of living are not as substantial as they seem. I have always felt a debt to France for this enrichment, but I was later to realise that personal insight and even courage are not the best weapons to cope with completely unforeseen (and not merely unconventional) challenges.

My first year ended well and in July 1933 I took two certificates in French Literature and Philology respectively, and I went back to Austria for the whole summer. At the *Burgtheater* I saw one of the most moving plays of my life, the first part of Goethe's *Faust* with its portrait of the demonic hero and his titanic striving for a life of pleasure, love and knowledge – memorable passages of which have stayed alive for me ever since. I also became a member of the municipal library, where I could find books on ancient Greek literature and many Viennese curiosities such as Einiger's dubious *Gender and Character* which purported to show how inferior women were in every respect. I also made many friends, including the bright young son and musical daughter of a charming middle-class family. I was not involved in politics in any way, but it was significant that I was taken to be a Social Democrat refugee by the porter of the building where I had my digs, largely I supposed because my German accent was northern.

I had developed such a taste for my studies that I applied to get my scholarship switched from Glasgow to Paris for the next year so that I might try my hand at securing the *Licence-ès-lettres* degree which needed four certificates. The application was approved and I was thus enabled to continue my studies in Paris which would be accepted as the equivalent of a year in Scotland. The obvious choice of subject was German and I had to engage in the exacting task of translating from

German into French. The students on these courses were quite different from those I had met the previous year. Many of them were young German Jewish refugees who sought sanctuary in France from the Hitler régime until they could see more clearly whether to venture back to Germany or emigrate. But the atmosphere in France and Germany had changed following Hitler's coming to power, and they were careful to avoid any discussion of the painful subject of politics. They were also reluctant to cut off their lifeline with Germany. Most of the students were middle-class and did not seem to have any marked political line. I only met one Communist among them, François Bondy, a Trotskyite, who became a well-known French journalist and ended up a prominent figure in an Italian anti-Communist movement which was sponsored by American funds. From him I gathered a fairly clear picture of what was going on in Germany. I also began to understand something of the involved controversies over reparations, and to see how unbridgeable was the gulf between French and German attitudes. Politics still hardly entered into my day-to-day life, but I did attend a meeting called on behalf of the German politician Thaelman, who had been imprisoned by the Nazis and on whose behalf an appeal was made for funds. The meeting shed no new light on the German situation and Thaelman was later freed on the understanding that he would withdraw from politics.

After I had completed the Sorbonne's degree course in July with two German certificates, I returned to Germany for the long summer vacation of 1934, cycling along the Rhine to Strasbourg, and saw for myself, with alarm, Hitler's rise to power and the impact of his totalitarian imprint on the country. In my diary I recorded meetings and conversations. One such conversation was with the father of Joseph Welter (whom I had met in Glasgow) who deplored the lack of discipline which had led to the unrest in Germany: 'Germany must have an army,' Herr Welter insisted. 'It is the right of every free-born man to defend himself, and Poland is making things difficult for us. There must be conscription. Yes, Germany must be armed.' A young Nazi I met told me that the Polish minority in Germany had almost disappeared, that the German minority in Czechoslovakia was well settled, but related terrible tales of the oppression of Germans in Lorraine, Estonia and Poland.

Regarding Hitler himself, reactions varied. Herr Welter thought that 'the Hitlerites are exploiting unemployment by great promises. He has reached his zenith and will decline.' A young man from Heidelberg felt that all political parties in Germany were out for money and that, 'Hitler wanted to make a bit of money and then clear out.' He described the National Socialists as 'a very tough gang who promise heaven and earth to the country'. The anti-Semitic attitude of the Nazis was clearly expressed by a young Nazi from Frankfurt whom I met in Aschaffenberg. He was well connected and had some fantastic ideas: the *Frankfurter Zeitung* was a Jewish rag, and when Hitler came to power it would have to be printed in Yiddish. All other parties apart from the National Socialists were to be suppressed. This aspect was summed up by Joseph Welter as 'the evils of the Jews. They are atheist, immoral, dishonest in business and anti-national. The Jews must go.'

In Koblenz I put up at a cheap hotel and visited the castle overlooking the junction of the Rhine and the Moselle where magnificent stretches of vineyards swept abruptly down to the river. I joined some men talking politics. One was a Nazi from Munich, but most were Communists. The Nazi was lame and one of the Communists was crook-backed, and I learned to my astonishment that nearly everyone was a *Kunde* or beggar. The jovial Nazi explained the technical terms of his very successful profession, and a florid Communist showed me his rosary – he was in the religious begging line! The Nazi started chaffing the Communist about their boozing capacities, but when more Communists arrived they voiced their opinions that Hitler had got his votes through lies and that his Nazi Party was full of mere jingoists. The first Communist complimented me on my German as being 'as good as a professor's' and another said I was certainly German or one of my parents was: I gave the first a glass of wine and the other I thanked.

These numerous conversations with Germans in their own language had in particular brought home to me their determination to remove the stigma of defeat embodied in the Versailles Treaty of 1919, and it was not long before I realised that this pent-up feeling of resentment constituted a serious threat to the democracies' moral values and to the stability of Europe. In addition, I saw that the Nazi system bore within itself a crude aggressiveness for which I, as an individualist and ardent defender of personal freedom, immediately developed a lasting hatred. My impressions proved that Hitler had massive support in restoring the battered self-confidence of his people as well as their discipline and enterprise. In my daily journal for August of that year I outlined:

> Comparison between Hitler & Mussolini & respective movements. Points of similarity obvious. Militarism, youth movement both parts of the nationalistic reaction against pacifism, internationalism & socialism at least – (*re* Hitler) against Marxism. However there were differences. In the case of Hitler the race was stressed. It alone made the nation. The will to power, to the self-preservation of the race in the mould of the nation was emphasized. Nietzsche & Darwin were the sources of his philosophy. In the case of Mussolini the nation was everything & it alone gave the race its validity. Mussolini was merely imprinting the old Roman idea of order on a nation which had not been disciplined.

I also recorded:

> Hitlerism seems to be merely an exploitation of the injustices sustained by Germany after the war, combined with the dishonest business control of the Jews and anger at the former government's incompetence. Nearly all the idealistic youth and the middle-class are in it. Big business, as everywhere in Germany, is behind it. It seems to be distinctly reactionary and militaristic, though it has no real programme.

When I got to Berlin I stayed with a Jewish family as *au pair* and English tutor to their son, and so met their circle of middle-class friends. I often accompanied them to the theatre and the opera and once saw a humorous *Cosi fan Tutte* in military costume. In German films I heard for the first time Jan Kiepura singing '*Heut Nacht oder nie*', and Beniamino Gigli singing '*Non ti scordar di me*'. I also profited through my day-to-day contacts with ordinary Germans, read German newspapers and listened to the German radio. On one chilling occasion, I saw Hitler pass by erect in his car saluting the crowds. But all this was not to remain on a theoretical level, for in 1938 I aided this same family to move to England by helping with the transfer of their money. I also gave a purely formal guarantee for their livelihood, which was the first step in enabling all three members of the family to emigrate to America.

*

<u>Article</u> 'Comparison between Hitler & Mussolini - & their respective movements. Points of similarity obvious. Militarism. youth movement both parts of the nationalistic reaction against pacifism. internationalism & socialism. at least (re Hitler) against Marxism. However there were differences. In the case of Hitler, the race was stressed. It alone made the nation. The will to power, to the self-preservation of the race in the world of the nation was emphasised. Nietzsche & Darwin were the sources of his philosophy. In the case of Mussolini the nation was everything & it alone gave the race its validity. Mussolini was merely imprinting the old Roman idea of order on a nation which had not yet been disciplined.

At the end of my final year of study in Paris I had intended to go back to Glasgow University and finish my Modern Languages degree, but my brother Alec suggested that I might sit for the Open Scholarship Examination at Cambridge. I had never before considered trying to aim as high as the famous English university, and had not even bothered to find out details about scholarships. My first reaction to the suggestion was one of hesitation for I imagined that I had not much chance of success against fierce competition from all over the country. However, my brother's encouragement made me reconsider the advantages of a prestigious 'made in Cambridge' degree, and I finally decided to make a special trip and take the exam. Luck was with me. I was asked about Molière and my enthusiasm for him so carried me away that my answer ran to fifteen pages. I was also happy to have a chance to indulge in my love for poetry, since in the written exam I had to translate the moving quatrain of François de Malherbe on the death of a friend's daughter. I still remember my version, which ran as follows:

But she was of the world, where beauty only knows
The saddest destiny.
A rose herself, she lived only as lives the rose,
A moment's brevity.

It seems that it was mainly because of my feeling for foreign languages that I came top of the list. At the oral exam I heard, in an audible whisper, the eminent Pascal scholar Professor William Stewart tell his colleague: 'It would be difficult to get better than that.' I felt that the reaction to my performance reflected a willingness to accept what was a liberal approach to another culture and this gave me hopes of fitting into the Cambridge atmosphere and of having a stimulating and profitable time in my studies. My Paris experience, in freeing any inner tension had, however, been a parting of the ways. My future was to lie outside Scotland (even if my background would underlie my evolution in later years) and thus my preference would always be for a more Latin reaction to the world.

THREE

Cambridge: My Flirtation with Communism

I arrived in Cambridge in the autumn of 1934, over a year after Hitler had come to power, and I was given rooms in New Court among the ancient buildings of Trinity College. My brother Alec, who was in his postgraduate year reading for a doctorate in Economics, profited from this by leaving his lodgings and sharing my rooms with me. This was very reassuring: I would not be living with a stranger – and perhaps at long last I would now have the chance of developing a closer relationship with him. I felt fortunate in having him to help me find my feet for I must admit that, though I was thrilled by my unexpected success in entering Cambridge, I was never to feel entirely at home there. I was taken aback by the prevailing authoritarianism which contrasted strongly with the free and informal life I had led in Paris. Regulations requiring undergraduates to be back in their rooms by 11 o'clock, to wear their gowns even when cycling to College from the railway station, and the system of fines made me feel that I was back at school.

However, the positive aspects of my new life were many and engaging. In particular, my eyes were opened to the vast wealth of art and music which was concentrated in so small an area. There were plays, concerts and films galore, so that it was sometimes a battle to find time to do some academic work. Above me on the same staircase lived such interesting people as George Painter, biographer of Gide and Proust, Paddy Costello, an ex-Catholic Communist, and James Klugmann, a Jewish Communist from Hampstead. Just below was a Research Fellow in Modern Languages named Anthony Blunt, to whom, however, I took an immediate dislike.

There was, of course, not the faintest trace of femininity at Trinity –

a most unnatural and stifling atmosphere. Women were virtually excluded from what was a distinctly homoerotic (as opposed to outright homosexual) male society. Sexual repression thickened the air, and the more energetic of the collegians found an outlet by resorting to London on their favourite express train, which was dubbed the 'Flying Fornicator'. This idea did not appeal to my more romantic nature, and my sexual experience remained nil. There were female students at women's colleges but when I invited one to tea, she immediately insisted that we would have to be chaperoned. Even dinner in Hall was a chilling experience, although the setting was splendid with Holbein's portrait of Henry VIII – founder of the college – over the High Table at the far end of the room.

I at once developed a close friendship with Etienne Tamboury, a young Frenchman whose father was a small manufacturer in the south of France. He had had a romantic flirtation with the Trotskyites, orthodox Communists having, he thought, strayed from the narrow path of Lenin's idealism. I fear that I diverted him from the straight and narrow path of his English studies since we had long discussions in French on every possible subject, including his extensive amorous experience, but this still left time for him to encourage me in my Molière research. My closest companion among the French students was Douglas Parmee, a handsome and socially successful man, who was an excellent French scholar.

Because of my *Licence-ès-lettres* from Paris I was dispensed from the first part of the normal three-year Cambridge Tripos. My general tutor was J. R. M. Butler of the well-known Cambridge family which included the young R. A. 'Rab' Butler of later political fame. My French tutor was Professor Henry Ashton, a genial Edwardian figure who had given up his chair at Vancouver to lecture at Cambridge. I have rarely known a Professor of such inspiration to his pupils and I was fortunate to come under his care. He was an excellent scholar who had produced, amongst other works, a carefully crafted piece on Molière; and it was in an essay for him on Molière's *Tartuffe* that I first developed my theory that the original version, now lost, was in three acts instead of the standard five. Here my inspiration was directly due to Dr Ashton's stimulating guidance, for this approach, which I have since developed, coincided with his own view – and was a very unpopular one in French academic circles.

Blunt was on the French teaching staff, but he was never my tutor, and my relations with him were distinctly frosty. He struck me as a typically English case of someone whose good knowledge of the French language (acquired through his living in France when his father was chaplain at the British Embassy in Paris), supposedly guaranteed an understanding of French literature. He had a confident and authoritative manner, a capacity for clear exposition and a remarkable facility of expression when lecturing on French literature or on his theories of the evolution of French painting or Marxist ideas in art history. It was not clear to me on what Blunt based his claim to rank as an expert in French literature, for he had no reputation or standing of any kind in French literary circles. He and I clashed on several questions of seventeenth-century literature and even on art. On one occasion he displayed a lamentable ignorance of the Spanish element in Corneille's plays. He knew only of *Le Cid*, as would any first year reader, and became very annoyed when I mentioned two other of Corneille's works. His rooms were impressive, enhanced by Poussin's 'Rebecca at the Well' which he had picked up in Paris at a bargain price; and he boasted a wide range of eminent social and literary acquaintances.

The German side of the faculty included a recently appointed lady professor whom I never met; Roy Pascal who, along with his wife, was a dedicated Communist; and a German refugee called Samuel whose lectures were professionally excellent but inefficiently presented. For me, however, the central figure was Professor Arthur Knight, known for his rather brusque manner, who would rattle through his carefully-prepared lectures so that no one could absorb them. For the first time in my academic life I had to write essays regularly, and I was thus enabled to study in depth various German philosophers, Goethe's political ideas, Hölderlin's superb and utterly inaccurate reconstruction of ancient Greece and Mörike's delightfully romantic poetry and his account of Mozart on his way to Prague. But most intriguing was the chance to explore certain novel fields which I had come across in Paris and Vienna, but had not had time or leisure to examine fully. There were, for example, the libertarian ideas on sex of Wilhelm Reich, whose central concept – which had unfortunately become entangled with all sorts of irrelevant undergrowth – was that sex should be looked on as a dynamic force and not as an evil to be thwarted and suppressed. Reich had unfortunately tried to marry his ideas to Marxist philosophy, with disastrous results.

Then there was the problem of the origin of Christianity. It was no novelty to maintain that St Paul's Hellenised approach had profoundly modified Christ's message and had transformed it into a mystery religion, thereby paving the way for the acceptance of the new faith by the Western world. But the new idea put forward by Goguel and Guignebert in France was that Christ was really a protagonist of Jewish independence against Roman rule, and that he had been put to death by the Romans as a rebel and not by the Jews as a religious heretic. However, by a neat piece of rewriting, the New Testament portrays the Jews as the villains of the piece, with the Roman ruler Pontius Pilate declaring that he finds no fault in this man. I was later to find this thesis developed with superb scholarship by the orthodox theologian, S.G.F. Brandon, though I was to hear friends dismiss the idea as an atheistic view.

I profited greatly from frequenting my brother's circle of research economists. One of the many authors who was to enrich my mind during my stay at Cambridge was the Italian thinker and economist, Vilfredo Pareto. He was in the realistic tradition of Machiavelli, and he now enjoys a well-deserved revival of interest. He appealed to me by his down-to-earth similes, and by the avoidance of an extreme realism which sometimes shocks moralistic thinkers. I considered him a welcome counter-weight to writers who operate in a void, and he taught me to look to the strength of the various forces in any situation before expressing an opinion on it.

However, perhaps the most significant development for me at this time was that I started to write poetry. The inspiration of my first effort was literary – a Corsican song in a French novel which begins:

If ever I should come to paradise and did not find you there
I would depart.

By a device which is as old as writing itself, I inverted the sentiment and, after describing the breakdown of the romance, concluded:

If ever I should come to paradise,
I would turn back again if you were there.

Poetry was then, as it would remain, an unconscious burst of song which often came to me in sleep or in that half-awakened state which is so propitious to fresh ideas. For all I know, it was as a reaction against my *milieu* that I started to write.

I noted at Cambridge the importance attached by most English students to convention and rank, which went well with a general hostility to, and ignorance of, continental ideas. There was only one point of view, and all other approaches were automatically rejected. I found the rigidity of this insular attitude to be a kind of ideological corset holding in check any resistance to external and subversive ideas. I was used to a much more relativist point of view, partly because of my experience in Europe, but also as a member of a small nation.

However other more important issues were beginning to obtrude themselves on the scene. There was a pervasive feeling that Britain was not moving forwards or playing its part on the international scene. Unemployment was rife, though I had the feeling that the University was largely insulated from these harsh economic realities. On the other hand, even the scions of affluent families were concerned about their career prospects, and it was widely realised that the Empire was in imminent danger of disintegrating. Though the industrial backwardness of the country was still not debated, there was no feeling of confident progress on that front, such as was to emerge with force once wartime needs for specialised arms and machine tools had to be satisfied.

Britain's diplomatic retreat in the face of Nazi expansionism, however, was widely felt, and it was here that Communism scored most heavily, since none of the other parties had a clear line. The feeling of staleness also made the novelty of Marxist doctrine, with its ready-made answers for all queries, appealing to students who lacked a forceful doctrine to oppose the new faith. This attraction was specially powerful for students from outside England, who were able to take a more detached view of the country's weaknesses, since they did not share the rigidly nationalistic view held by their English colleagues. Thus, converts to Communism were specially numerous from the Dominions and from the continent. Paddy Costello, a New Zealander, was a well-known radical, while the Canadian, Herbert Norman, was said to 'brush his teeth' with Communism. In the 1930s, there was an influx of students from less affluent strata, but I never had the impression that converts were more numerous from these groups than from the better-heeled ones. I put this difference down to the latter's less intense concern for material problems, whereas English students of more modest origin had their hands full with simply staying afloat in prosperous surroundings whilst securing an economic niche for themselves once their studies were over.

I doubt whether anybody would now be interested in this pre-war Communist phase of the student body were it not that a certain number of converts became involved in espionage. At the time, the existence of the KGB at Cambridge was unthinkable even to those interested in Communism, with the exception of those actually initiated. During my two years there, I met two men who subsequently became notorious as KGB agents – Blunt and Klugmann.

Blunt was a well-known Communist who made no secret of his political views. I saw little of him and had no discussions with him on Communism: were he to have had an influence on me it would certainly have been unfavourable. Only in 1979 did I learn that, as part of the KGB network, he had played an important role in orchestrating my recruitment and had therefore greatly influenced my future. James Klugmann was a modern languages student whose views on French literature and history I found stimulating, although our main point of contact was a joint conviction that Nazism had to be resisted. He was the most prominent Party member at Trinity and it was he who brought me into the Communist circle; and it was probably through him that John Cornford – later killed in the Spanish Civil War – asked me to join the Party, which I never did. This was my first contact with organised Communism and I felt impelled to look into it, as it was the only Party in Britain determined to oppose the expansion of Nazism. On the continent I had developed a passionate revolt against the crudeness and intolerance of the Nazi Party; but in England I had found that the only people who took the menace seriously were the Communists.

So, after a time, I began to attend various meetings. I at no point participated in the cell's activities, except at these meetings, and we were not a ginger group to judge from the frequent strictures of the cell leader Ewart, whose father was diplomatic correspondent on the *Daily Herald*, a Labour newspaper. Ideologically, there was no meeting of minds, since I have never taken to Hegel's philosophy or to Marxist economics. My abiding inclination was more for the humanity of Hume and Diderot, which had recently been tempered by my cultivation of Pareto whose insistence on the importance of power in international equations was a great help in enabling me to interpret the strategy of both Hitler and Stalin. Also, I had no sympathy for the agitation of workers which seemed to me pointless. Nor was I stirred by the Communist attitude to birth control or indeed by their approach to women's issues generally. On the other hand, I readily accepted the Russian policy of collective security, and militated in favour of an alliance with Russia against Germany.

I gradually acquainted myself with the Communist attitude towards Germany. In 1935 I talked with Klugmann about the Saarland referendum whereby the French had hoped that the Saar would be detached from Germany. The Nazis had won an overwhelming victory and the Saar remained German. I expressed to him my opposition to the French Communists, but asked why they had joined with the other political parties and done so badly in the voting. He replied sensibly but, I thought, prosaically, by pointing out that if they had gone in by themselves they might well have done worse.

The Communists were very active in a number of Cambridge clubs in which they were predominant and where they spread their propaganda. I got involved, as a fellow traveller, in two of them. One was an economics group which met in Blunt's rooms, and which may have been just an ad hoc rather than a regular affair. It was attended by Maurice Dobb, a prominent Marxist economist, and by the American, Michael Straight (later revealed as a KGB recruit whose disclosures to the FBI in 1964 led to Blunt's confession). I remember making sceptical remarks at a meeting about surplus value and other Marxist economic dogmas, but Straight did not seem to have registered my reaction, and later he even swallowed Klugmann's tale that I was such a profound believer that I went underground and sat for the Foreign Office exam on KGB instructions.

The other club was a pacifist society, where I witnessed the standard Communist tactic of infiltrating non-communist groups and taking them over. Some Party members joined the pacifists and then, when their position was deemed sufficiently strong, undermined and finally absorbed the society. The one memorable meeting I attended was addressed by Dr Glover, the same psychoanalyst who had once calmed my fears as a child. This time he really alarmed me, for he assured us that all that was needed to keep Hitler at bay was an absence of fear. I cannot say that I shed any tears over that society's disappearance.

My contact with the Communists held for only eight months, since the essential bond had been anti-Nazi, and the Party tended to focus more on the conclusion of a political alliance with Russia regardless of, or even in spite of, its ideology. I soon grew disillusioned with its shrill rhetoric about class relations and its emphasis on anti-employer, pro-worker policies.

The most obvious field of activity for me was, of course, the Modern Languages Club, which being inspired by Blunt, usually also met in his rooms. The club soon ceased to exist, but I well remember the one meeting I attended at which Blunt gave a convincing lecture on the application of Marxist theory to art. The two periods for which these views were most skilfully exploited were the Italian Renaissance and French Impressionism. In the former case, he stressed the clarity and simplicity of outline and structure corresponding, he asserted, to the views of the new middle class, which was replacing the feudal system. The Impressionists, for their part, reflected the retreat of the declining bourgeoisie from a harsh economic reality. When asked what course he favoured at the present moment, he replied tersely: the proletariat.

Blunt's desire for power was overwhelming and it took, among other forms, that of a thirst for recognition. In fact, even when he had formally withdrawn from his KGB connection, he built up a very powerful position of authority in the art world in which he was able to blight the careers of those daring to disagree with him. These unfortunate scholars based their conclusions about the authenticity of art on actual details dated and controlled, whereas Blunt insisted that it was connoisseurship which counted, thus in effect saying that father knows best. He also put through certain curious deals in the art world, which have given rise to a good deal of discussion about fraud and which are described in *Drawn to Trouble* by a collaborator of his, Eric Hebborn.

I am convinced that Blunt's KGB activities must have given him an immense thrill, as he was able to play a key role himself, as well as indirectly manipulating others. He brought under his control as recruits

John with Persian greyhound in Rome, 1989 (© Fiorenzo Niccoli).

The author as a baby in his mother's arms, surrounded by the Cairncross clan (brother Alec in the sailor suit).

The author's parents, Alexander Kirkland Cairncross and Elisabeth Wishart Cairncross.

John with his elder brother Alec, growing up in Lesmahagow, 1921.

Main Street pre-war Lesmahagow. On the left is Cairncross and Menzies Ironmonger's shop next to the Royal Hotel; across the road is the Commercial Hotel.

The author, aged 14, at Hamilton Academy.

The author aged 19.

With brothers Alec, Andrew and friend rambling in the Scottish Highlands in 1932.

The author in his first year at the Sorbonne in Paris, 1932.

John Cairncross at Cambridge.

(*Opposite*) Official portrait of John Cairncross on appointment to the Foreign Office.

John and Gabriella Oppenheim marry at the Kensington Registrar Office, London, 1951.

mainly lower-class students, such as Leo Long, who were gratified to find themselves rubbing shoulders with members of the élite. Blunt seemingly wanted to create a new form of the class system, and by joining the secret society of the KGB he placed himself above the social grades of English society. He would have expected to have been sitting on top had the revolution ever materialised. There is no more angry snob – for he was a snob *par excellence* – than one who has been snubbed, as he had been, by his socially superior relatives. Blunt also seemed to have visions of ruling the roost in the art world later on, when he prophesied that, after the great upheaval, there would be jam for all.

There is really no difference between the power complex as applied to art or as applied to the world of espionage. For when one penetrates behind the screen of words, the pattern is the same in both spheres, and the curious thesis put forward by George Steiner in his famous *New Yorker* article (*Reflections*, 8 December, 1980) that there was a contrast between Blunt's ideal world of art and the sordid activity of espionage, does not stand up to analysis. Blunt was a natural disciple of Marx, drawing on the master's theories to underpin his own views. And he was thus able to deliver them with an authority which he would otherwise not have dared display. A leopard does not change his spots, however red they may be. I have a suspicion that Blunt's initial interest in dogmatic Marxist theory was triggered by his study of the Alberti case, around which his book on Renaissance art is built. I was once told by a Viennese friend that Blunt took his views on Renaissance art from two Austrian scholars whose names I have forgotten (a son who died early and whose theories were then developed by his father).

It is in any case a pity that the question of Blunt and art was not discussed in more depth in John Costello's biography *Mask of Treachery*, for it might have thrown further light on the central question of Blunt's motives and his devotion to art. Whatever the feebleness of his theories on Poussin, so completely demolished by the vastly superior critic Sir Dennis Mahon, Blunt was certainly deeply involved in his subject. But there is another channel by which Blunt's passion for art must have influenced his conversion to Communism and his desire to be revenged on the existing social pattern. This was the radical emphasis on sports in the public schools and their hatred of art. So much has been written about education as practised in the élite schools of England that it is hardly necessary to elaborate.

There is, finally, the question of his homosexuality. It is not quite true that homosexuality was central to espionage, as the historian Robert Cecil maintains, for it seemed to pervade the whole of upper-class English society, and is no more common in Intelligence circles than elsewhere, although there it was kept even more secret. It is true, however, that in England the public schools fostered a certain kind of homoeroticism blended with an aristocratic anti-art heartiness, which must have given the final offence to Blunt the aesthete. Blunt's homosexuality no doubt helped him to develop a capacity for leading a double life, though not perhaps in a mastery of blackmailing techniques. Certainly, homosexuality must have had some influence on security within the KGB's network, as Blunt, Burgess and Maclean were drawn together by circumstances. But it is obviously easier to attack the citadel of orthodoxy from within, and this is exactly what Blunt was able to do from his position of privilege.

As the end of my studies drew near I sat my final exams, gained my BA with first class honours and was faced for the first time with the problem of earning my living. My brother's circle of research economists had been on the fringe of my main interests and I had been fortunate in making the acquaintance of the now distinguished economist, Sir Hans Singer, whose remarkable talent for explaining complex economic theories in simple language was to be of great value to me in the Civil Service exams I was shortly to take.

At Cambridge I had drifted into Communism without joining the Party, and by March 1936 I had sidled out. When I went down in June, I imagined that my Communist connections would remain merely academic, but I was soon to learn how wrong I was.

FOUR

The Foreign Office: The KGB Trap

On leaving Cambridge, my preference would have been for an academic career, but no offer was made to me, not even of a research scholarship. This was due, no doubt, to my not having taken the proper preparatory measures while I was studying for Finals. I thought that my academic record, and my obvious interest in research, were sufficient to stimulate the authorities to offer me a grant. Professor Harry Ashton, I knew, would have backed me strongly, but I waited in vain for an expression of interest. I should, I imagine, have contacted the right people and chatted them up, but when nothing came I began to think of finding some other job, as I had no intention of further exploiting the generosity of my parents. The most attractive alternative was the Civil Service, which would offer a steady job, always provided that I passed the stiff entrance examination. But, before giving up my dreams of academic glory, I had taken the precaution of consulting a modern languages lecturer at Trinity, Dr Harmer, with whom I had no previous connection and who was therefore likely to be completely unbiased. I explained my predicament to him, and his reaction was immediate: 'Go in for the Civil Service,' he urged. Thus, when the summer holidays came round and I had finished the Cambridge Tripos in modern languages, I spent some three months in a rented room in Paddington preparing for the lengthy September exam for the Foreign Office, as well as for the slightly different version of that test for the Home Civil Service. My more affluent friends did their training at crammers, whose professional job it was to prepare candidates for the exam, but I both distrusted these and, in any case, could not afford them. I laid in a stock of Horlicks malted milk to help keep up the necessary energy and I indulged in about ten hours' continuous sleep every night. But my main device was to get hold of the exam papers for previous years, for the type and number of questions are bound to be limited. Even if one is not lucky enough to hit on exactly the earlier version of the question in the current exam, one can form a fairly good idea of the knowledge demanded of the candidate by the examining board.

I was on the whole well prepared on the language side, and I was sure that there were few candidates likely to outdo me in that field. On economics, I was less well prepared, but I had been lucky enough to be given the essence of Keynes in five lessons by Hans Singer. His assistance enabled me to get through one of the economics papers which, luckily, was devoted to Keynesian theory, and I was familiar enough with the topics in the other paper. But luck was with me generally, for just before going in to sit one of the history papers, I had run through an account of the political situation in France in 1848 and to my delight was able to produce a satisfactory reply to one of the questions.

Immediately after the exam, which was spread over three weeks, I left for Berlin to await the results with my friends the Sänger family whose son I had tutored in 1934. There I received a telegram from my family

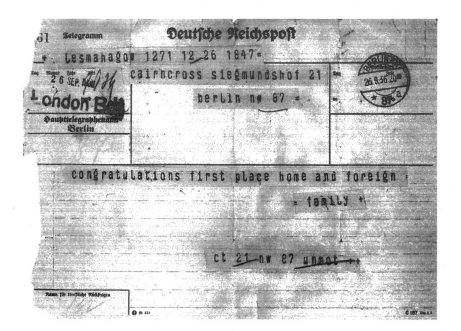

who gave me the good news that I had come out first in both exams. I was overjoyed because I had frankly regarded my chances of success as about one in three. However my trials were not over yet: there was still the *viva voce*, the oral exam, to be passed.

Back in London, the chairman of the examining board was a senior Foreign Office official. The other members included two impressive ladies, of whose identity I was unaware. I did not go down well, and when I was asked about my impressions of the situation in Germany, I explained that I had visited the country frequently, that I was apprehensive about the danger of German expansionism and also that some of my friends had been adversely affected by the Nazi régime. I had the impression that this was not the answer the board expected, since they did not seem to relish my acknowledgement of a personal involvement in the issue: they were perhaps more at home with a detached analysis of 'British interests'.

One of the next questions concerned a poem by A. E. Housman, about the mercenaries in ancient Rome who 'saved the sum of things for pay'. There had recently been a severe criticism of the quality and morality of this poem by Cyril Connolly in a leftist paper, the *New Statesman*, on which I was asked to comment. I made two blunders: I admitted that I shared the critic's views, and added that the poet seemed to me to simplify and dispose of a complex issue about the decline of the ancient world in nothing more than a rhetorical flourish. The poet's works had a special appeal to English ears and sensibilities, but to me they appeared somewhat affected or over-pretty, and I made the mistake of voicing my opinion to the examining board.

To my considerable surprise, I again topped the list of candidates, and the doctors, after some hesitation over the sight of my left eye, pronounced me fit to join the Foreign Office. I had plumped for the Diplomatic Service in preference to the other possibilities because I looked forward to spending part of my time abroad, and also because I had not realised the predominantly social duties of an embassy *attaché*, such as bridge, golf and parties outside office hours.

I started my duties as a Third Secretary in the American Department at the Foreign Office in October 1936 at a salary of £275 a year (less taxes). This posed a very practical problem since I could not live in London within that income, however modestly. Fortunately, I was subsidised from home and was just able to manage. I was also lucky in

(X 6958/6958/504)   FOREIGN OFFICE, S.W.1.

                                     14th November, 1956.

        Sir,

                I transmit to you herewith a Commission which

        The King has been graciously pleased to grant to you under

        the Royal Sign Manual and Signet, constituting and appointing

        you to be a Third Secretary in His Majesty's Diplomatic

        Service or Foreign Office.

                        I am,

                            Sir,

                        Your obedient Servant,

                    (For the Secretary of State)

being offered a berth in a quiet suburban house on Gunterstone Road, W14. This I shared with an agreeable fellow civil servant, Eric Wagstaff, who worked in the Board of Trade. Always cheerful, he was passionate about music, especially opera. We each had our own room on the second floor and telephone calls were received on the flat owner's phone. Outings into town were few and far between and initially I liked this calm and withdrawn life, as the exam and the previous tests at Cambridge had tired me out. I worked happily at home on various aspects of my reconstruction of Molière's original version of *Tartuffe*. I did not have many friends, but the few people I still saw from my Cambridge days were Professor Ashton and James Klugmann, whom I would meet every so often.

When I first entered the Foreign Office building, I was very impressed by the whole aura of tradition and influence which it exuded. It was not a particularly beautiful edifice, but it was finely situated. It lay at one end of the short strip of Downing Street, and at the other it looked out on the spacious expanse of St James's Park. In Downing Street are concentrated, in a very small space, the ministries that make up the heart of the British Establishment, with the exception of the Bank of England and the City. Between that street and Whitehall, which is at right angles to it, there is on the same side as the Foreign Office what used to be the Dominions, Colonies and India Offices, which have since been absorbed by the Foreign Office. On the other side is the famous No. 10, the Prime Minister's residence. At the corner with Whitehall, there is the old Treasury building with its splendid eighteenth-century facade and its rabbit-warren interior.

In those days, there was only rarely any question of an identity card and least of all in the Foreign Office, where each member was known personally to the porters. They not only knew each member by sight, but discriminated between them according to whether they fitted into the category of the established type. Thus when, a few days later, I told the porter on duty that I was expecting a visit from a Mr Cowan, a Canadian friend of Scots origin, his benign reply was that he would make a note of 'Mr Cohen's' impending visit. I was thus credited with a cockney accent and in a kindly spirit immediately placed in a lower rank.

In spite of potential difficulties that I might have in assimilating the new atmosphere, I had the impression that I would eventually fit in, and at first I seemed to be succeeding. I felt that, unexpectedly, I had arrived in a prestigious, if alien, world. However, the difference in background was to constitute an insuperable barrier. It was not so much a question of my approach to politics, as one of attitudes. There was too big a gap between my continental, informal and egalitarian mentality, which I have always felt comfortable with, and the Foreign Office world, at least at that time, with its feudal presuppositions. I had the usual introductory talk with the Personnel Officer, who was most pleasant and who made a particular point of telling me, for which I was grateful, 'We don't say "Sir".' He clearly thought that I would sprinkle my conversation liberally with this term signifying recognition of seniority or class superiority, in which he was vastly mistaken, for I have always regarded the use of this form of address as a superfluous term of submission.

I had just turned 23 but I was so small that I had to buy a hassock to bring myself up to the right level of the desk in the American Department, which was a quiet backwater, at least at my humble level. My work was concerned with the territorial claims by Honduras on the British colony of the same name, and a demand by Venezuela for the surrender of a rock off the coast of British Guyana. I was not concerned with top level policy issues and not at all involved in high level diplomacy, so I usually kept my mouth shut. However, at the wedding of a colleague (for which I had to invest in a morning coat) I was responsible for purchasing and preparing the tea, being the most junior official. When Sir Robert Craigie, the Under- Secretary, came out to my astonishment with a strong endorsement of Germany's claim for colonies – which I strongly opposed on both political and ethnic grounds – I ventured tactlessly to express my scepticism of his opinion. After this terrible bloomer I was rebuked by a senior colleague for my arrogance, but surprisingly was not hauled over the coals more sharply.

Today there is a tendency to forget this sombre epoch in Britain's history, which caused such traumatic crises of conscience. The period will be familiar to many, but perhaps, given the victorious outcome of the war, younger readers may not be aware of the poor figure cut by Britain up to 1939. The Nazi threat was already in the air when I went up to Cambridge in 1934 and grew steadily more alarming as Britain, with her Empire in decline, remained disarmed, both spiritually and materially. The whole country was blinded by complacency and a firmly rooted conviction in the power of her moral superiority. She was furthermore determined not to become involved in continental entanglements and was thus condemned to virtual isolation. Thus in the mid-1930s, Britain, weakened by the policy of disarmament consistently practised (despite the protests of the military) since the First World War, found herself faced with the threat of Hitler's increasing expansionism and her only way out would be the sacrifice of other countries, thereby only whetting the Nazi appetite.

At that time the Chancellor of the Exchequer, Neville Chamberlain, had been more concerned with balancing his budget than with building up the nation's defence. And the Prime Minister, Stanley Baldwin, ignoring the threat, pursued a policy of business as usual. In 1936, Germany was allowed to take over the Rhineland, which historically had always been her jumping-off point for the invasion of France. In May 1937, when Chamberlain took over power from Baldwin, the situation became even more serious. Hitler continued to build up his air force, while Chamberlain adopted, with missionary zeal, a policy of appeasement, which amounted in fact to one of retreat. Entirely ignorant of European conditions and with no experience of foreign policy, he dealt with Hitler – as with a troublesome trade union leader – by negotiation. He felt that Hitler, after sowing his wild oats, would settle down and stop causing trouble if he were approached diplomatically and if some of his territorial claims were satisfied. Opposed to an alliance with Russia, the Prime Minister yielded at every turn to German pressure, thereby strengthening Hitler's position. He also neglected the anti-Hitler feeling in the German army. He thus gave up one position after another, which was to lead in 1938 to the dismemberment and subsequent occupation of Czechoslovakia, a strong pro-Western power. The only clear way of defeating German expansionism in 1938 would have been the removal of Hitler from power.

Public opinion in Britain was largely indifferent to fascism in Italy, Germany and, later, in Spain and was divided between an inert majority eager to avoid war at almost any cost and a more realistic minority, led by Winston Churchill who was then out of power and widely regarded as a dangerous extremist and maverick. Inside the Cabinet there were a number of ministers who were broadly in favour of resistance, such as Duncan Sandys and Duff Cooper, but Chamberlain rode roughshod over their objections and tried to discredit them, speciously representing them as warmongers who were rashly propelling Britain towards a clash.

If Chamberlain's policy created the illusion that, if only the West were prepared to make concessions, a solution would be possible. Some people in the Foreign Office were even prepared to envisage a division of power between Britain and Germany, the one retaining its Empire and the other taking over Europe. I remember talking with people who were well prepared to meet Germany's claims if, for instance, Hitler were replaced by the more jovial Hermann Goering. In contrast to the general complacency in Britain, Russia's outspoken unwillingness to accept Nazism exercised an increasing appeal and created an opening for Communist propaganda and Marxist theory, which otherwise would have fallen flat. I and my like-minded contemporaries found the German idealistic philosophy underlying the Marxist creed completely indigestible. It was a period which generated excessive retreat from reality in Britain and often inspired extreme ideas and reactions. This, too, was a time when danger, nationalism and political ideology propelled many ordinary men and women into a maelstrom. It was this climate of imminent war which led to my becoming involved with the KGB.

During my studies at Cambridge I had never smelled the slightest whiff of KGB operations; as far as I was concerned the Russian intelligence agency might have existed on another planet. However, when I joined the Foreign Office, it crossed my mind that the Communists' interest in me was likely to increase as the Foreign Office was obviously a prominent target for penetration. From being a bright if unconventional student, I had become a potentially interesting source of information, but, as I had heard that the CPGB (Communist Party of Great Britain) had its own intelligence organisation, it was from that quarter that I anticipated an approach. I knew that any connection with the Party, if it became known, might lead to my flirtation with the Communists being dug up, with possibly unfavourable implications for my career.

I did not have to wait long to see my expectations justified. Soon after I had started work in my new job, I was rung up by Roy Pascal, my former tutor in German at Cambridge whom I had known as a prominent Communist. He suggested lunch at Lyons Corner House, a good and cheap eatery near Marble Arch. We chatted for a few minutes on various topics including the rapid spread of Communism in Britain and, after we had been mellowed by a satisfying meal, he produced the expected suggestion that I should be put in touch with a friend of his who would keep me abreast of what he termed 'political developments'. The implications of the offer, although not hinted at, were clear: I was to be enrolled in one way or another in an intelligence-gathering organisation. I listened carefully, but made no move to follow up the offer. This was exactly the type of approach I had feared.

A similar approach was made at about the same time, but it was probably less carefully orchestrated. Neither approach I have concluded now, had KGB overtones. I was invited to attend meetings of an informal group on current affairs at the house of Sir Walter Layton, the Managing Director of a Liberal newspaper, the *News Chronicle*, whose son David was an acquaintance of mine. At one of these meetings, Ewart, who had been the leader of the Trinity College cell of the Party, got into conversation with me and asked me bluntly if I had anything to report. I fobbed him off with general news items and, after a while, I dropped out of the circle. Much later, when Czechoslovakia had become Communist, it appeared that MI5 had taken an interest in this circle. I would imagine that this was because one of the Layton daughters had married a Czech and was resident in her adopted country. I am convinced that the KGB knew nothing of these approaches and, if they did, would strongly have disapproved of them. They regarded the CPGB's intelligence group as bungling amateurs. Later, one of my Russian handlers would be scathing in his comments on the arrest and sentencing of Douglas Springhall, a senior Party official who had been in contact with Captain Ormond Uren, a member of the Special Operations Executive (SOE), the wartime sabotage organisation. Both were charged with espionage in October 1943 and given long prison sentences.

And so, as time went by, I began to feel that all would be plain sailing, and such was indeed the case. What I did not suspect was that a far more powerful Russian protagonist was already at work, and that much of my apparent security was due to the care they were taking in preparing to try and recruit me.

I had the impression that I was passing muster in my work, for early in February 1937 my office life was to become more stimulating when I was transferred to the more active Western Department, which included Spain. I had been fortunate in visiting that country in April 1936 when, having learned the language from some Spanish refugees, I had taken a train from Paris to Barcelona and found a pleasant *pensión* on the Ramblas, run by a Frenchman. The Republic had been set up for some time and on 14 April, the national holiday, I watched the troops marching to cries of 'Viva la Republica'. I found Barcelona a curiously un-Spanish city, being the capital of Catalonia and open to French influence, and the most go-ahead city in the whole country. From Valencia I went out to a family whose address had been given to me by a Spanish friend and there experienced the warmth of Spanish hospitality. I had imprudently lent a large portion of my small capital to a German in Paris who promised to send it to Madrid. Upon arriving, I immediately went to the post office but no money had come for me, nor had the letter I had been expecting with money from home. I had to tell the hotel owner, at the end of my stay, that I had no money. He was very nice about it and was, of course, reimbursed in due course. So, with my last pesetas I bought a bun and took the long train journey back to Paris, fortified on the way by some draughts of wine proffered by the pleasant Spanish occupants of my carriage. Although this trip had not greatly enlarged my knowledge of the political problems of the country, it had been a valuable experience and good practice for my new post in the Spanish section.

My supervising officer there was a reserved official, (Sir) William Montagu-Pollock, who held liberal views and seemed someone with whom I could easily get on. But, for some reason I never understood, I did not hit it off with him. My main job was to handle the release of British or British-protected people detained by the Franco authorities in exchange for right-wing persons held by the Republicans. In this assignment I was fairly successful, thanks to the splendid efforts of our agent in Franco's Spain, Señor Milanes, whom I nicknamed Señor Milagros ('Mr Miracles'). The most famous figure he managed to rescue, probably from execution, was the writer, Arthur Koestler, who was exchanged for the wife of a distinguished Nationalist pilot. I have no idea how the operation developed, but at least I can claim to have pressed for action after the Department had rejected further intervention as hopeless. I was elated when Koestler, still looking worn and tired, turned up with his young fiancée to thank us for our help.

It was in the Spanish Section that I first made the acquaintance of my new colleague and immediate superior, who was much the same age as I, and who had entered the Diplomatic Service a year earlier. Donald Maclean seated opposite, was a tall, mild-mannered figure. He was clearly an up-and-coming official, highly intelligent, most competent in his work and always friendly, though he never expressed strong views either in conversation or on paper. He rarely discussed foreign politics, and the only opinion I heard him express was the need for Britain to re-arm. I would never have suspected such a congenial type of engaging in KGB activities, but there was a remark I remember which might have prompted me to imagine some out-of-the-way activity, which was to the effect that it was inconvenient to have only electric or central heating as there was nowhere to burn papers. At the time, of course, I had no context to fit such a remark into. We never developed a close relationship. He enjoyed dining out in the small cosy restaurants in Soho and seeing the latest plays. The nearest we got to familiarity was to see a play together, *The Golden Boy*, which was about a boxer who loses his good looks in the ring. Towards the end of my stint with the Department Maclean confided to me that I did not make the right impression because I was too spontaneous and oblivious of conventional behaviour: it was not so much a question of having the wrong views, though this was also noted, as not coming from the right background.

The atmosphere in the Spanish Section was fairly balanced, but I witnessed at first-hand the effect of the sham policy of non-intervention in Spain. There was little inclination to favour either side, with just a few sympathising with the Republicans and the majority non-committal. The most partisan was the Under-Secretary in charge of supervising the Department, Sir George Mounsey. It was alleged by a future ambassador to the Vatican that he was spat upon by everyone because he was mildly pro-Franco, a highly biased version of the situation. The Head of Department, (Sir) Walter Roberts, was middle of the road, while Sir William Montagu-Pollock, was convinced that the Republicans had more popular support. The fact was that Britain considered the Spanish Civil War a nuisance, kept going by the Russians for no good reason, and was concerned above all to see it finished, being happily resigned to see Spain fall into the hands of the German-Italian axis. The extent to which a show of force would have paid off was demonstrated by the attacks made by the Royal Navy on the unknown submarines sinking British and other vessels bringing arms to Spain. Once it was clear that Britain was reacting, the sinking of British ships mysteriously ceased.

It was at about this time when I started going to parties and meeting people that I made the acquaintance of Guy Burgess. At Cambridge he had left a somewhat dubious reputation behind him as a brilliant, effervescent but unreliable character. Several of my contemporaries had warned me against him, including, significantly, James Klugmann. I cannot remember precisely where I met Burgess, but it was probably at one of the many parties which he attended, for he was a great socialiser. From then on, we met occasionally for drinks and it became obvious that he was beginning to cultivate me discreetly, although at the time it was not at all clear why. I have no doubt, looking back, that the KGB had arranged to bring us together. He moved in exalted circles, was well-informed, and expressed himself with ease and wit on a wide range of subjects. I must admit that I was somewhat flattered by his attention. Incidentally, he gave me an idea of how I was regarded in the office: favourably, it appeared, though I suspected that this was largely the afterglow of my success in the Foreign Office exam.

Burgess asked me to 'meet a few people', as the standard English formula has it, all of whom turned out to be quite distinguished. One of them was (Sir) Harold Nicolson MP, a former Foreign Office man and a writer, whose famous novel, *Public Faces*, gives a masterly picture of political and diplomatic life. Another regular guest was Wolfgang zu Putlitz, a senior German diplomat, now said to have been a lover of Burgess's and an agent working for both Britain and Russia. Subsequently, I learned that he had been one of Churchill's main sources of information about the strengthening of the *Luftwaffe*. He had left London for The Hague, but was airlifted to safety by SIS when he fell under suspicion. After the war he settled in Communist East Germany.

Burgess next invited me to meet the poet Louis MacNeice, in Blunt's rooms at Trinity College, Cambridge, one Sunday. The bait was well chosen, for my interest in the modern literary world was widely known, and it was realised that, as an outsider, without a high-level introduction, there was scant hope of my ever meeting such an eminent figure. This skilful KGB manoeuvre exemplified the agency's adept use of all the cards at its disposal. Blunt, the moving spirit and the main strategist in the KGB's recruiting network at Cambridge, on that occasion made no secret of his political views, but these were always set against an artistic and cultural background. There was a complete absence of any political debate, and it was perhaps because of this rarefied atmosphere that I cannot remember a single word of the conversation that afternoon.

In our discussions hitherto, Burgess had not touched on politics, but now the stage was set. When, after the meeting, we took the train back to London together, he brought the conversation round to the international situation and asked me what I felt about it. I had no hesitation in telling him that war with Germany seemed almost inevitable; Franco, an ally of the Axis powers, was taking over Spain aided by a sham policy of non-intervention. I said that unless Britain pressed on with re-armament and formed a military alliance with at least France and Russia, we would find ourselves waging a war for which we were ill-prepared in every way, and would not be able to stand up to an aggressive and militarist Germany. Burgess nodded sagely, but made no comment. He was apparently much less reserved with others, for he told a fellow anti-Nazi, the Welsh academic, Goronwy Rees, of our conversation and boasted that he had recruited me to the KGB during that trip.

The next move in the game took place in Paris. When I told Burgess I was contemplating a short trip, he said that he too had occasion to go over on business, and it was without enthusiasm that I agreed to meet him there. I felt it was something of an intrusion, as Paris was in a way my own personal centre for evasion from a specifically English atmosphere. On the ferry from Dover to Calais, I was seasick and I arrived at my usual hotel in the Latin Quarter somewhat the worse for wear. Burgess had told me, as if he were referring to a well-known landmark such as the Ritz, that we were to meet at a homosexual café called *Le Sélect*. (Previously, he had never so much as hinted at his homosexual tendencies. Indeed, he seemed to have been making an effort in our conversation to put me at ease on that point. I remember once walking over to his London flat, which was in the same district as mine, with the intention of leaving a message as I could get no reply on the telephone. After ringing the bell, I was on the point of leaving, when he appeared, obviously roused from sleep, and apologised for having been so long. 'I was with a girl,' he said sheepishly.) When, with a certain embarrassment, I started my inquiries about the whereabouts of *Le Sélect*, I was met with blank stares, and I was therefore only too ready to let the matter drop and get in touch with my regular friends, such as Etienne Tamboury whom I had met at Cambridge and who was now installed in Paris as a fully-fledged lawyer. Etienne was to introduce me to many interesting people such as a client of his whom I shall call 'Wilhelm', an ex-*Luftwaffe* pilot who was in danger of being expelled from France. He had claimed to have invented a new device for detecting the presence of enemy aircraft. Later he had been brought to Britain by the Air Ministry and on the outbreak of war he was interned. I would hear no more of him until I was questioned about him on my joining the SIS.

I must admit that the main source of my reluctance to delve deeper into the question of finding *Le Sélect* was the homosexual element and so, given the after-effects of my seasickness, I decided to retire to bed and try to recover a *joie de vivre* more appropriate to the Parisian milieu. I never showed up and, as Burgess had not told me where he was staying, I never contacted him. Nor did he know where I was putting up and so was unable to get in touch with me. Little did I anticipate that my failure to meet up with Burgess was to have marked consequences for me. Burgess was stalking me for the KGB. I was the poor scholarship boy who was to be dazzled by his social glamour and important social contacts. I am sure that, in Paris, he planned to confront me and somehow clinch matters. My impression was confirmed by his very annoyed reaction the next time he saw me after the aborted meeting, and that afterwards he rarely spoke to me again. But any appeal from Burgess to join the secret society of the KGB would have struck me as offensive, for nothing had led me to imagine that Burgess was a Communist agent. What is more, if he and Blunt, the Etonian socialite and the 'brilliant' art critic and Fellow of Trinity, were really steeped in Communist dogma, neither had given me the slightest hint of a commitment to stopping the expansion of Nazi aggression.

After the startling news of Burgess's defection in May 1951, I was to give the matter a good deal of thought and considered the possibility that he might have planned to turn up in Paris accompanied by a KGB agent, but I could not believe that he would have been willing to so jeopardise himself. According to revelations from the KGB's archives, Burgess often acted on his own initiative and was a menace to that organisation's strict security. I cannot imagine where an encounter would have led, but it would certainly have had unfortunate repercussions for me. Perhaps Burgess was trying to recruit his first sub-agent, but I cannot imagine a professional Russian intelligence officer happily appearing in a notorious Paris homosexual club. Perhaps Burgess would have promised me social backing and help in my career in exchange for my loyalty to the KGB, but it would have been the wrong card to play. As I have never taken kindly to condescension, I would surely have lost my temper at finding myself in the very compromising situation of knowing about Burgess's KGB connection. My reaction might have given him grounds for suspecting that I would report his involvement in that vast underground network of subversion and intrigue.

How Burgess might have been prepared for such an emergency is beyond me. Perhaps he thought he had threatening cards up his sleeve to use against me, and maybe that was why he chose a homosexual haunt. I later learned that his position at the time was an official of Section D, the clandestine sabotage agency preparing for war, with an emphasis on anti-Nazi propaganda. I have since speculated that he might somehow have tried to show that I had been involved directly in some of these covert activities. His only other course would have been blackmail – bringing my earlier Communist association to the attention of the authorities, perhaps embroidered with a number of frills, just to make his story more effective. It is possible that, if indeed they knew of the arranged meeting, the KGB took my non-appearance at *Le Sélect* as an indication that the Burgess approach to me had been the wrong one. They therefore decided to have recourse to James Klugmann, the only Communist activist from Cambridge with whom I had kept in touch. I used to meet him roughly every six weeks, partly to share our interest in French literature; but I also had at the back of my mind the idea that continuing contact with him might be useful in keeping tabs on any Party developments at Cambridge likely to have repercussions on my career – for I was not at all keen for my former Communist associations to become known. This was a serious error on my part, for it enabled the KGB to take me by surprise.

It was in May 1937, while I was still with the Spanish Department and beginning to spread my wings, that I was trapped into an appointment with the KGB. In the actual recruitment, four men were involved: James Klugmann, who lured me to the meeting; Otto, the KGB man to whom he introduced me, and Burgess and Blunt, who had, without my knowledge, secretly stage-managed the operation. Klugmann had arranged for the two of us to meet in the evening at Regent's Park, a spacious and delightful spot close to the West End where, he probably calculated, we would not be recognised or disturbed. I had dined early in a small Italian restaurant in Soho and was looking forward to a pleasant stroll in a green setting. I arrived at our 7 o'clock *rendezvous* at one of the park entrances to find Klugmann waiting for me and we made our way into a part of the grounds with a fair number of trees. It was still light, but there were not many people around. I noticed that Klugmann was not his usual smiling, chatty self. My instinct of unease was not mistaken, for suddenly there emerged from behind the trees a short, stocky figure aged around forty, whom Klugmann introduced to me as Otto. Thereupon, Klugmann promptly disappeared without even daring to give me a furtive look – and I did not see him again until almost thirty years later, when I unsuccessfully confronted him with his deception.

We shook hands and Otto said: 'I believe you've been to Germany often and know the country well.' He then pointed out that the British Government were cooperating with Hitler, and appealed to my anti-Nazi convictions and the need for all peace-loving people to unite against the danger from Germany. It was not difficult to guess what was happening. I was appalled at my predicament, and my first reaction was to fold-up inside. As I had little to contribute to the conversation and hardly spoke, my hot-headed anger gradually give way to a fatalistic calm and my survival instincts emerged as I began to take in his words. Otto was clearly an experienced practitioner who gave the impression of keeping power in reserve and he made his pitch with great smoothness and skill. There was no mention of Marxist theory, the class struggle or dialectical materialism. Nor, of course, was there the slightest reference to espionage. But 'cooperation' in this sense was implicit in all his remarks. In particular, he held out the prospect of my rising to the top of the Diplomatic Service should the Communists ever take power in Britain. After all, he observed, the Czarist diplomat Georgi Chicherin had been converted to Communism and had become the Soviet Foreign Minister. This curious carrot was the only inducement the KGB ever offered me; but as I regarded Britain as the last country likely to embrace Communism, I managed (even in the circumstances) an inward smile.

But, at the same time, I recognised the cold-blooded tactical deception of the KGB which savoured of another and more dreadful world. It was certainly an abrupt leap from the academic discussions I had been enjoying with Klugmann. The welter of emotions and arguments which flashed through my mind reduced me to a state of momentary shock, particularly when I remembered the KGB's reputation for ruthlessness (given their treatment of statesmen such as Nikolai Bukharin and the cream of the Red Army). I resented the crudeness and deviousness of Klugmann, who had acted as a catspaw, for the KGB would never have been able to catch me off my guard but for his trickery. My first encounter with Otto lasted less than half an hour and ended with my agreeing to meet him again, but nothing more. I made my way out of the park, got home in a taxi, arriving in a disturbed condition, and took a strong glass of whisky. I then had a light snack and sank into bed, exhausted by the strain. I was eager to work in any way I could for the alliance between Russia and Britain against Nazism – but not as a Soviet agent. There was no question of my taking part in any campaign to help change the régime in Britain, or indeed to work against Britain in any way. Any decision to maintain contact would need to be based on my right to take only such action as was compatible with the anti-Nazi line I had adhered to for the last few years: I would never surrender my independence of judgement.

Naturally I was never told Otto's real name, but we now know he was Arnold Deutsch, one of a group of Soviet undercover agents, mostly of central European or German origin called 'illegals' because they operated with false passports and 'legends' and therefore without diplomatic protection. His accent immediately suggested that he was German rather than Central European and we often spoke German, though his English was creditable. I also guessed that he was Jewish, and hinted at this by referring to Hitler's persecution of that community, and he confirmed my guess by his immediate and clearly personal acknowledgement of my attitude. I gathered that Otto must have worked in Austria where, because he was Jewish, he had presumably moved after Hitler came to power. His origin would explain why, as he later indicated, he had spent some time in Austria before coming to England, for the anti-Semitic attacks came later in that country. The 'illegals' were deeply distrusted by Stalin and were largely eliminated in 1937, to be replaced by Soviet Embassy staff, but the recruitment of the Oxford and Cambridge networks probably would never have been so successful but for their skill, flexibility and cosmopolitan ways. In particular, they carefully abstained from the obvious use of force, pressure, threats or power-plays. And, in the prevailing climate, they reaped a rich harvest. Later the embassy staff merely carried on where they had left off.

Clearly there must have been mutual misinformation on a considerable scale between the four men involved in my recruitment – Blunt, Burgess, Klugmann and Otto. I suspect that Klugmann had argued that I was suitable KGB material since I had not broken with him even after my appointment to the Foreign Office. Guy Burgess, I guess, did not intervene strongly in the discussion since his own approach had failed, but he probably emphasised my strong concern, expressed on our train journey from Cambridge, for the need for military strength, including an alliance with Russia. Blunt, who hardly knew me, but who I suppose had planned the operation on that day when I had met Louis MacNeice in his rooms, was presumably convinced by these two that it was possible to make a direct if dangerous attempt to win me over. It is worth stating here that in 1952, when I came under MI5's suspicion for the first time, a note was prepared by a Security Service source (and all leads point to Blunt) asserting that I had given every indication of being a convinced Communist until I ended my studies. It is possible that Blunt had come to the wrong conclusion about my position, but it is more likely that he read the writing on the wall portending his own imminent exposure, and wanted to strengthen the security authorities' belief in him as a reliable source. Otto, for his part, may have chipped in with his strange Chicherin ploy on his own initiative, which seems a carry-over of Burgess's original strategy of offering a humble scholarship boy social acceptance and career advancement.

The plotters had counted on the effects of a surprise attack on my youth and on my scholarly otherworldliness, a condition which despite my clear ideas on politics had never crossed the line of demarcation from ideas to actions. But we did not come to terms easily and my first meeting with Otto ended in a stand-off rather than an arrangement for collaboration. Indeed, my whole relationship with the KGB can be described as a fragile balancing act on a tightrope. There had been no explicit request for me to act as an agent, nor any threat to take measures against me if I did not agree; but certainly the KGB would have interpreted any lengthy procrastination on my part as a decision to denounce them. The contrast between a rapid decision taken under pressure and the formal exposition of the factors underlying that decision is not just rationalisation after the event or the reaction of a cold and calculating character. There was no saying what they would do if I hesitated, for I was in a position to blow Otto, undoubtedly one of their most important agents. Klugmann would also be put at risk, though he had been regarded until then as merely an ardent intellectual propagandist. He could no doubt have lied his way out of the situation just as, when I finally confronted him thirty years afterwards, he was to shrug off any responsibility for his shifty approach.

As for myself, I surmised that the authorities would recoil in horror were they to learn that the KGB had approached an official of the Foreign Office, however junior. They were probably just as ignorant as I of the depth of KGB penetration in Britain, and immediately would have dug into my Cambridge background. Unlike Donald Maclean, who had admitted his Communist associations at his oral examination for the Foreign Office, and had been commended for his frankness, I would not have been given the same exoneration and my student activities would then be viewed in a much more sinister light. Maclean was a member of the élite, whereas I was the son of a modest Scottish shopkeeper. I was certain to be dismissed and, what is more, I would find it almost impossible to obtain another job since potential employers would immediately wish to know why I left such a prestigious post so abruptly. It was even possible that I would have been pressured to act as a double agent and as I regarded Chamberlain's policy as betraying the national interest and dividing the nation, I would not have felt justified in becoming an indirect instrument of that policy. Thus, to report the KGB's approach to my superiors in the Foreign Office would have been formally correct but would have meant not only the end of my career, but virtually the end of anything resembling a normal existence, even at the humblest level. If the choice was between full collaboration, which I never contemplated, and denouncing Otto and thereby facing my own ruin, I decided to play it safe and not report the approach. Nevertheless, I left the meeting with certain clear inner reservations.

My recruitment took place against a background of a radically deteriorating international situation, fraught with tension and the danger of war. I might have found it easier to decide which course to pursue had there been an open and well-focused discussion about appeasement, instead of a virtual driving underground of the essential political issues. Had I been able, for example, to turn to a Churchillian political party, it is just possible that I would have adopted a less dangerous course. My views, which were held by only a minority in Britain, were not uncommon among those familiar with Germany and the German problem, but I knew even then that anything short of a direct contact at a very high level would not have given me the guidance and support which I so badly needed. There was no political party with which I felt in sympathy: both the Labour and Liberal parties opposed the Defence Estimates needed to sink our teeth into a more courageous policy almost until the outbreak of war, while the Conservatives, fearful of Communist agitation and hesitant to stand up to Nazi expansionism, tended to look on Hitler as a useful bully-boy. Churchill did raise his voice to warn against the danger Britain was running into by its spineless policy *vis-à-vis* the Nazis, but, as I have said, he was a lone figure, widely regarded as a maverick or, as John Colville defined him, bearing in mind his mother's American origins, a 'half-breed and an adventurer'. If political debate in Britain had gone underground, in France the issues were brought out crudely but clearly. The forces calling for an anti-Nazi policy were denounced not only as warmongers but in the pay of the Communists and the Jews.

The considerations present in my mind at that decisive moment in Regent's Park were even more complex and conflicting, for they were not dominated by fear alone, but included a strong element of idealism. I imagined that I could play a useful part in the coming struggle against German expansionism. As an individualist with high ideals and a good grasp of the international political situation, I saw a positive reason for not flatly rejecting contact with the Russians. Since I doubted the West's capacity to stand up to Germany's military might, I felt that it was essential for a resistance movement to be organised and to that end there seemed to be some point in keeping a line open to Russia, especially through a secure underground agency. For Russia, with all its resources and vast territory, would probably be able to hold out against a German invasion, and ultimately win through. In the short term, unless a more powerful combination of forces was organised, Britain might well be invaded or reduced to the level of a satellite by a collaborationist government. This prospect would have seemed unbalanced to most people in England in 1937, but when, three years later, the *Luftwaffe* was poised across the Channel to destroy the Royal Air Force prior to invasion, the danger could not be dismissed as fanciful. Nor would my calculations have seemed so unrealistic to a member of the French Resistance after that country's defeat in 1940 when, as de Gaulle was to find, hope of liberation lay in help from an outside ally.

I felt that the British Communists were not capable of forming such a resistance movement. Indeed, the English character does not move along these lines as does, say, the Irish. Russia, on the contrary, had both the strategic base outside the country and the experience in clandestine activities to develop an underground movement. All my continental friends with knowledge in this field were unanimous as to the need for experience and skill. I had talked at Cambridge with a German woman involved in this type of work, and in France with Italians who belonged to the non-Communist movement *Giustizia e Liberta*. They had impressed me with the need for careful and professional preparation: otherwise the result would always be high losses, both in effort and success as well as in lives. Looking back, this attitude seems like a generous and speculative illusion, but my experiences on the continent had convinced me of the strength of German willpower and drive and I was eager to seize upon what may sound a desperate project in defence against a future of complete isolation. As in the First World War, Russia was needed to be able to force a fight on two fronts if it came to hostilities. Already weakened by the strain of the First World War, Britain under Chamberlain's leadership might, I feared, arrive at an understanding with Germany.

Some of today's espionage experts and molehunters appear convinced that I remained in contact with the KGB solely for ideological reasons. Far from being disgruntled because of my so-called working-class origins, I was riding high. I had gone much further than I had ever expected, and entered the portals of one of the élite centres of administrative power with prospects of a bright future ahead of me. This was the last moment at which I would have felt impelled to protest against the social order. My one preoccupation was to prepare for the effects of a disastrous foreign policy. I was not likely to run such considerable risks simply from a messianic conviction, but I did feel unable to sit back and allow disaster to overtake Europe and possibly Britain without playing a part, however modest, in attempting to resist it.

Together with the prospects of future glory, Otto had taken pains in his argument to minimise the risks I would run if I agreed to work for his agency. He swore that in Germany, where he had operated before Hitler's rise to power, none of his agents had betrayed their political faith. I did not make the obvious comment, especially as I was merely speculating about his experience, that this record might not have been maintained under the much more drastic repression of the political opposition after the Nazis had come to power. He assured me that I would be released if I ever wanted to withdraw from this situation, and gave me the example of one of his agents in Britain who had married a bourgeois wife and decided to cease his entanglement with the KGB. (I later identified this person as the Welsh academic Goronwy Rees.)

Given the horrendous political purges in Russia at that time, it was asking a good deal of me to accept these reassurances blindly. Otto's possible fate, his liquidation in Moscow so soon after our meeting, would certainly have made me even more sceptical. However, the fear of Russian vengeance and intrigue if I did not go along with Otto also made me temporise. I was pulled in the same direction both by the unspoken threat of blackmail and by Otto's assurances, however unconvincing, that I would be able to cut the connection if the situation became intolerable. In the case of espionage, however, any contact is usually binding, and marginal involvement is impossible, but it was only much later that I realised that this was so.

I promised to remain in touch with Otto and my life henceforth followed a sequence of unexpected twists and turns which showed that my hopes of pursuing my own line were going to be fraught with difficulties and that I had committed myself to threading my way through a treacherous minefield.

Since I was a new and untried agent, my running-in period was fairly lengthy. The KGB wanted to be sure of my reliability and Otto, like all Soviet agents, was a fervent believer in security precautions in testing new recruits. He seemed to have a fondness for meeting in parks rather than remote suburbs and I, too, preferred this whenever weather permitted. As an 'illegal' operating without embassy cover, there would be no question of diplomatic immunity if he were arrested; he would be tried like any ordinary citizen. He therefore never bothered to advise me of what tale to tell if we were seen together. Otto's practices, in contrast to my later experiences with other KGB handlers, reflected a more informal approach to personal security. He even once told me that during the days of the Popular Front in Paris, he could almost operate openly.

On the other hand, I have wondered whether our initial meetings had not been tailed by the KGB (perhaps to see if I was having Otto spied upon). For on one occasion, he told me that I had not been sufficiently careful in taking precautions and had been tailed to our previous meeting. However, as he never gave me any technical guidance on the point, I doubt whether I was very effective in throwing off any shadowers I may have had.

Much has been written by others about my first encounter with Otto, and many of the comments which he is alleged to have made to me are quite fictitious, and probably go back to Blunt's confession to MI5 in 1964. For example, the reported remark that I should improve my pronunciation of English would have been much more likely to have come from an Englishman, rather than from a German-born controller. Similarly, the advice Otto is supposed to have given me not to marry a bourgeois wife sounds like a distortion of his statement about Goronwy Rees.

Our monthly meetings went on, with no real impact on my office life, until September, four months after the meeting in Regent's Park. As I guessed later, the KGB had probably been in something of a hurry to recruit me since, like any careful organisation, it planned ahead. They knew that juniors in the Foreign Service were usually posted to an embassy abroad after two years' service and assumed that Maclean was due to be transferred to an embassy around September 1937. (We now know from files in the KGB's archives that I was to be his replacement, since they had no Soviet source in that office.) Hence the KGB's direct attempt to recruit me in May. The origin of my 'active' recruitment only appeared in later information on Maclean released by the KGB: for some reason, Maclean's posting was delayed for a year, but as the machinery had been set in motion, I was invited by Otto to provide him with 'any interesting data' I came across. These, in fact, were not very great because the department dealt only with Spain and no secret information arose at that time. The meetings at which I delivered an envelope containing information from the Foreign Office were few and far between. I confined this information to the minimum and, for example, supplied a paper relating to Italian violations of the non-intervention agreement in Spain which only contained facts generally known. I was thus providing information already available to the KGB through Maclean, duplicating material of no value. I provided no further data until after the Germans invaded Russia.

Soon after my recruitment, Otto, who had no doubt been primed on social affairs by such experts as Blunt and Burgess, stressed the importance of my moving from lodgings in the suburbs to a more central address. This suggestion came as a surprise to me for I had always thought that such an aim would be well beyond my means. In very general and discreet terms, Otto insisted that it was of the utmost importance and I realised that pressure would be applied were I to refuse this idea. After careful inquiries, I was able to find accommodation at a tolerable rent in Warwick Square SW1, close to Victoria Station and neighbouring the more fashionable district of Belgravia. My new flat of three rooms was modest, but overlooked gardens with a tennis court. There was no lift and the bathroom was on the staircase landing, but it was a decent address, and not far from my office. It did not involve much extra expenditure but it was still almost beyond my means and this was covered by a slight subsidy from home. The furniture was of the simplest, and all I needed were two beds, two tables, some chairs and a sofa which were provided for me by Mrs Ashton, my former Professor's wife, at a nominal price. This move to Pimlico was a great step forward for my private life as I could now ask friends in for a drink or a girlfriend to supper. What was more, I could go to one of the many films showing in the West End without too much anxiety about catching the last train home. There were also a couple of excellent, inexpensive Italian restaurants in the neighbourhood to which I could treat myself or even a friend from time to time without making a huge hole in my budget.

I have been accused of regularly receiving expenses, a term which is usually put in inverted commas, during what is referred to as my 'KGB career'. It has been my misfortune that the molehunters got around to my case at a time when mercenary espionage had been the rule for over thirty-five years, and this has tainted their attitude about my motives. I have never denied accepting funds from my controller in my first year in the Foreign Office. At that time diplomats were expected to have a private income, and they may still be. I had none, but I was requested by Otto to join the Travellers Club, to which many members of the Foreign Office belonged. There are clubs in all countries, but I doubt if they have the same importance as they do in London. Failure to belong to a club of some standing meant that I might not be able to entertain properly, a necessity for maintaining one's standing in the Foreign Office.

Poverty is indeed relative. As a boy at home, I never felt deprived, for

I was living in a small, compact society where everyone had much the same needs and income but, in my new surroundings, things were quite different. I must admit that I viewed the prospect of failure because of lack of financial means with considerable dismay. It was not for me a question of status, but of the personal satisfaction of filling a post of great responsibility and of being a source of pride to the family which had constantly backed me and had been so ambitious for my advancement.

Otto, however, did not press me, as a condition of financial help, to supply information, and had I been earning more I would have foregone any aid. The Russians continued to offer money to me at regular intervals, but I only accepted when there was a real emergency, such as the moment when I needed expensive dental treatment. It is also often said that the Russians offer money in order to compromise their agents and prevent them from deserting the cause. I must say, without any intention of presenting them in a favourable light, that they never used the financial weapon against me. They clearly regarded me as an investment, whereby I would eventually be in a position to provide them with information, though what their attitude would have been had they known about my reservations I cannot say. Like most intelligence organisations, they were pragmatic and interested only in results.

My discussions with Otto on politics were few and far between, and completely uninteresting, but he admired the Austrian Communist Party for the soundness of its slogans and the correctness of its line, even though it was never a power in the country. In a conversation with the Cambridge communist hardliner Paddy Costello, I had once criticised Stalin's ruthless collectivisation of Russian farms and his decapitation of the Red Army. Otto must have heard about these remarks, for he chided me: 'But look what he's done for them,' which he seemed to think was enough to silence any adverse comment. Since anyone with reservations about Stalin was taken to be a follower of Trotsky, Otto treated me to a lecture on the difference between the two Russian leaders. Stalin, I was told, saw the world as it really was, while Trotsky viewed it through a mist of fantasy. (I was informed much later, by Peter Wright, that Costello had been a KGB agent, so presumably this was how Otto had learned of my dangerous comments.) But my association with Otto was brief and he was soon caught up in the turmoil of a sweeping change in Soviet intelligence policy. Although I was never informed of Otto's precise fate, I had always assumed that he was one of the victims of Stalin's purge, but the latest evidence suggests he died at sea during the war. Either way, my suspicion then that he had been liquidated was all the more valid if it is true that Otto was a disciple of Wilhelm Reich, the advocate of sexual freedom who had made the valiant but unsuccessful attempt to merge Marxist and Freudian principles. This kind of approach was anathema to orthodox Communists and, if Otto was really a devotee of Reich, it was inevitable that Stalin, who only accepted true believers, would eliminate him.

Towards the end of 1937 I was transferred to the Central, or German, Department of the Foreign Office, headed by Sir William (later Lord) Strang. He was a Scot of modest social origins like myself, although infinitely more capable, and one who seldom went beyond the most cautious statements on policy matters. He went along with Chamberlain's line of appeasing Germany and sacrificing Czechoslovakia, consistently recommending this passive policy, though not as explicitly as did our Ambassador in Berlin, Sir Neville Henderson. In my view he was the perfect bureaucrat and owed his rapid success to this combination of qualities and defects. On the other hand, I was happy to note that there were other members of the department who took an active interest in stimulating efforts to strengthen British aircraft by agitating for the purchase of Bofors guns.

The Central Department was at the heart of the drama as the European political struggle was played out in the stream of telegrams from Berlin and Prague. I had little to do there during this period leading up to Munich, as all the work was practically conducted by Chamberlain himself, whose iron control of the Cabinet and the Conservative Party was reflected in the small hand-written sheets of instructions which arrived almost daily and which determined policy – effectively reducing the Foreign Office to a cypher. My experience was essentially that of a spectator of the events leading up to the betrayal of Czechoslovakia, and I watched with impotent rage the battle being lost as those small sheets of paper, with their neatly-written sentences of instructions, flitted across our desks.

At roughly this time, in the midst of the general KGB turmoil, Otto was recalled to Moscow, but before leaving he introduced me to his successor, a Russian with distinctly Slavic features. This was Henry, whose real name was Anatoli Gorsky and who was already working in a minor post at the Russian Embassy. My impression of him contrasted sharply with his predecessor and this change significantly affected my relationship with the KGB. I had experienced no barrier with Otto, who had a pleasant and polished personality, like many continental intellectuals I had met on my trips abroad, and whose ease in establishing contact must have stood him in good stead in his work. I am sure that Henry immediately regarded me as an unbeliever. In contrast to Otto, it also seemed to be his habit to keep his distance from his agents, and that distance must have been even greater in my case. Almost as soon as we met he left for a lengthy period of training in Moscow and he stayed away for about a year. During his absence I was edged out of the Foreign Office.

I had made no impact in the Central Department, partly because there would have been no role for a junior in its high-level operations and partly because I was totally out of sympathy with the Government line. I suppose it would have looked amiss if I had not at least been given a try in the Foreign Office, since I had ranked top in the entrance exam, but in the end one either belonged, or one did not. I had been told by one of the examiners, who later became the head of the Foreign Office, that he had not thought I would fit in, but that I might be good on paper. Unfortunately, they said, this had not proved to be the case so there would be little option but to find another berth for me. I was also gently informed by Strang that I did not have the art of writing either letters or drafts. This has always perplexed me for in every other office in which I have worked I have always been sought out for my drafting ability. My two years in the Foreign Office had been a great experience, but I felt that my only contribution had been, as a junior member of the American department, to serve the tea and through my Treasury contacts, to obtain modern telephones to replace the heavy, anachronistic ones then in use.

Accordingly, in December 1938, I transferred to the Treasury where the staff were very much of my own type, forming a meritocracy in that key department of the Civil Service.

FIVE

Henry and the Molotov–Ribbentrop Pact

My move from the Foreign Office after only two years must have been a shock to the KGB's *Rezidentura* in London, since they had been counting on me to replace Maclean. Moreover, my work at the Treasury was almost entirely of a non-secret nature, which meant a sharp drop in my potential usefulness to the KGB.

During Henry's long absence in Moscow, however, an incident occurred in London which was to be far more damaging to me than my Russian involvement. Guy Burgess contacted me in July 1939 and said that he was working for a secret British agency (which was true) and was in touch with some anti-Nazi German generals linked with an underground broadcasting network (which was untrue). He told me that he badly needed information for them on British intentions towards Poland, but was unable to get this from the Foreign Office for bureaucratic – and probably also personal – reasons. Having left the Foreign Office by that time, I had no access to diplomatic information, but I said I would undertake to speak to some of my former colleagues, especially as I was intensely interested in the question myself. Burgess insisted that I could not be expected to entertain my friends without lunching them and gave me £20 for expenses out of his own pocket, and I gave him a receipt because he said he might manage to get the cash back from his office. Following my talks with friends and colleagues such as John Colville, I assembled a series of notes, with some rather general indications, which did not go much beyond what could be culled from the columns of *The Times*. I also provided a personal description of my 'sources' designed to enable the recipient of my notes to make some kind of assessment of their reliability. (It was later suggested by Peter Wright in *Spycatcher* that with these 'pen portraits'

I was talent-spotting for the KGB.) Just as I was preparing to type my notes at home the lights failed, and so I took a candle and wrote them by hand. (They were, of course, not on Treasury paper.) When I gave Burgess the notes, I asked that he not forget to return them but, in spite of his promise to do so, with his usual carelessness he did not, saying he had mislaid them. I was disturbed at this failure and dropped him, not speaking to him again except at the occasional dinner party with mutual friends.

It was at such a dinner party given by the Halperns that I saw him again and he was rather cool. Alexander Halpern, a fairly well-known lawyer of Russian origin, had been a minister in Kerensky's liberal revolutionary government until it was overthrown by the Bolsheviks in November 1917. His wife Salomé was a famous beauty, a tall semi-Georgian who had inherited the physical attributes of that race – and had been celebrated by a famous Russian poet. She moved in a select *émigré* circle which included Madame Arpels of *Van Cleef et Arpels*, jewellers in Paris, and Moura Budberg, who had been smuggled out of communist Russia by British secret agent Robert Bruce Lockhart and who was high up in Alexander Korda's film enterprises. Salomé's salon also included such interesting characters as Raymond Picard (later an eminent Sorbonne professor who became a close friend), Freddie Ayer, the philosopher, whom I also came across later in wartime Intelligence, 'Pussy' Deakin, the first wife of William Deakin (who collaborated on Churchill's memoirs), and Isaiah Berlin who, on the evening in question, told a host of riotous jokes. I only recall his version of the motto 'Watch and pray' which he had reduced to 'Watch', and I was subsequently to have the most ample reason to subscribe to his revised version of that proverb. Burgess and I were not seated together and we only exchanged a bit of small talk. He also (possibly on KGB instructions) no longer made any effort to cultivate me. When Henry finally came back to London he took me to task quite severely for having given my notes to Burgess and warned me to avoid him in the future.

I now realise the extent of my naiveté in my dealings with Burgess, for it is well known that these notes (which I am convinced he did not even use), were found in his trunk after his defection to Moscow in 1951. Had I been a little less credulous, I might also have spotted the deception of my expenses 'from his own pocket'. In extenuation of my simplicity, it should be stressed that there was a proliferation of curious secret agencies at the time, and there was no clear awareness of them or of their operations and finances. It must also be remembered that the West was on the verge of war, and that the whole of Europe was seething with conspiracy and suspicion. All the countries involved, including Germany, were eager to obtain some idea of their opponents' moves, but in spite of their efforts, none of them guessed the outcome correctly.

After the incident with Burgess, I continued working quietly in the Treasury, wondering why there was still no news about negotiations being carried out in Moscow for a pact between Russia and the Allies. These negotiations had been first diplomatic and then, for the last few weeks, concerned with arriving at a military understanding. It was towards the end of August that the explosive news of the Molotov-Ribbentrop Pact reached me and I was as surprised as the next man for I had not realised that the Allies were capable of bringing about such a disaster. Chamberlain had been naïvely convinced that Russia and Germany would never join forces because of their ideological differences, as if Russia would always put the purity of its Marxist doctrines above national interest. British public opinion had been convinced, in a passive sort of spirit, that if the Allies were kind enough to bring Russia, which had hitherto been something of a leper in international affairs, into the charmed circle of higher politics, it would be flattered and an agreement between them would be reached. This illusion was reflected in a cartoon which appeared in *Reynolds News*, a left-wing paper. It showed an irate lady in front of the cage of a Russian bear declaiming, 'No. No bun until you have signed the Pact with us.' A more realistic position was taken by the *Evening Standard* in a leader which appeared even before the news of the Pact and which, with heavy irony, portrayed the Politburo, the supreme Russian policy-making body, concluding its session by singing 'God save the King' – as if Russia were concerned only to save the West's bacon and did not have its own frontiers to defend.

I, on the other hand, suffered from the opposite illusion, which was that Britain and Russia were bound to end up on the same side, since they could not face Germany separately and their mutual survival depended on it. I remember having lunch with a Canadian banking friend, who was misguided enough to imagine that I had access to informed circles, but I was at a complete loss to explain the catastrophic news. And yet, if one went back over the events of the previous six months, the inevitability of this Pact stared one in the face.

For Britain's leadership 1939 had been a year of waiting, and this eventually led to a direct clash between Daladier, the French Prime Minister, and Halifax, the British Foreign Secretary. In March, Czechoslovakia ceased to exist as an independent power when Prague was occupied by German troops. British public opinion which had welcomed the Munich agreement with hosannas now shrank with revulsion. Chamberlain had panicked, and, with the zeal of the reformed drunkard (as historian A. J. P. Taylor puts it), showed the same incompetence in blundering into an agreement with Poland as he had displayed in ruthlessly betraying Czechoslovakia six months earlier. He offered, unasked, a non-reciprocal treaty of alliance to Poland, which guaranteed its sovereignty but was strategically not worth the paper it was written on. Moreover, he was as diligent in complying with the wishes of the arrogant Polish leader, Joseph Beck, as he had been in constantly thwarting the Czech leader Eduard Beneš.

The pressure for negotiations with Russia, voiced by such figures as Churchill and Lloyd George, now became irresistible. Chamberlain unwillingly gave in and talks were started in Moscow at ambassadorial level in mid-April. At this point I had relaxed, for the need for the alliance was so transparent that it was widely assumed, despite the distrust of the Soviets in some English quarters, that the talks were bound to succeed. As early as 3 May, however, hardly impressed with the progress of the talks, the Russians replaced the accommodating pro-Western Litvinof with the pedantic and aggressive Molotov, second only to Stalin in the Soviet hierarchy, as Foreign Commissar. By raising the status of its Foreign Minister, Russia, after many years of exile signalled that it was ready to re-enter the arena of international diplomacy, and that there would be no more free lunches for the West. On 23 July, Molotov decided that progress might be faster if the diplomatic subtleties were left till later and military aspects given priority. A Franco-British delegation was quickly assembled and dispatched – but by sea, without any sign of haste, arriving in the Soviet Union on 10 August.

This sorry tale of the fiasco of the Anglo-French-Soviet talks is told in full by General André Beaufre of the French delegation. It shows that the Allies had no real intention of coming to an understanding, but were only concerned to improve their bargaining position with Hitler over Poland. The delegation itself was relatively low-level and, without a letter of accreditation, had no power to come to an agreement. The figures given for available Allied forces, and especially the tiny numbers of British troops to be stationed on the Western Front, left the Russians speechless: the size of the armies which the West was prepared to keep lined up against the Germans was quoted as only forty divisions – which struck the Russians as totally insufficient to pin down a large mass of German forces.

Another stumbling block was the refusal of the Allies to allow the Russians, in the event of a German attack on Poland or on one of the Baltic states, to intervene militarily. The Allies adopted a view in favour of the moral right of these countries to decide for themselves if they were in danger, thereby putting Soviet assistance on tap. There was, inevitably, widespread scepticism about the genuineness of this argument: as Voroshilov, the Soviet Marshal, put it, the Russians had to implore the small states to be allowed to come to their aid. The West, indeed, felt that there was no danger of Russia and Germany coming to terms because of their violent ideological disagreement. In this they were wrong: both Stalin and Hitler were past masters in *Realpolitik*. And so, from delay to delay, discussions continued until 23 August, when Russia, determined not to be left bearing the brunt of Hitler's imminent attack, signed a pact with Germany, which meant that Hitler was now freed from the danger of fighting on two fronts, besides being assured of essential supplies such as oil.

In Beaufre's opinion, Russia had been interested in concluding an alliance with the Allies almost up to the last minute. When it became clear that there was a stalemate, the Soviets lent a willing ear to the German proposals. Ribbentrop, the German Foreign Minister, was ready and willing to pay the price, and the deal was concluded in under a week. The pact was in essence an improvised affair, and the surprising aspect of the agreement was why the Russians waited so long – for they ran the risk of the German army advancing eastwards after invading Poland.

The ignorance and stupidity of the Chamberlain-dominated Allies had resulted in the most inept diplomatic negotiations since those between England and the American rebels 200 years earlier, making war inevitable in conditions which were little short of desperate. It was distressing to read later that Chamberlain accused the Russians of ending the negotiations which he claimed the Allies were conducting in good faith, as if a country which had been quibbling for four months over petty issues was really only yielding to political pressure in negotiating at all.

The French had wanted a military alliance but their last-minute attempt to secure a defensive treaty proved too late. And it is ironical that Stalin should have been ready to sacrifice the support of Communist Parties abroad, whereas Chamberlain excluded Russian support, essential on any strategic reasoning, on ideological grounds. As it was, the Russian invasion of Poland, once war was declared by Britain on 3 September, barred the advance of German troops to the old Polish frontier, and to that extent marked a territorial gain for the Allies.

But, going back to my own position, this turn of events was disastrous for my plans, which now lay in ruins and made nonsense of my forecasts. I was convinced that the two new confederates would fall out and that Hitler would inevitably turn on the Russians after he had settled accounts with the West: but for the moment I had to soldier on in the highly uncomfortable position of being in touch with a friend of our enemy, with the danger of a German invasion of Britain far greater than before. It was a horrible situation while it lasted.

It was soon after the unfortunate Pact between Russia and Germany that in January 1940, some ten months after our first meeting, Henry returned. The formula that had been agreed on before his departure was carried out exactly: I would turn up on the first Saturday of each month at 5 o'clock at Piccadilly Circus: he would ask me the way to the Strand Hotel. After a few moments, I was then to catch up with him and follow him by Underground a considerable way out to the suburbs and double back in order to make sure I was not being followed. I had no difficulty in recognising him when he finally re-appeared: his impeccable clothes, the unfailing formal hat (Otto had always gone unhatted), and the round, moonlike bespectacled face allowed no mistake. I never knew for sure, but his sartorial elegance certainly suggested that he was based at the Soviet Embassy. On one occasion, while waiting at our meeting place outside a restaurant, I had looked in to see Henry talking to some English acquaintances. Afterwards, he reminded me of the need to observe all the outward proprieties in his role as 'the perfect foreign gentleman'. His instructions were always that, if I was spotted in his company, I was to say that he was a Czech engineer. Otto, who had been far more informal all round, never took such precautions.

Henry's immediate concern was to discover whether my departure from the Foreign Office was caused by suspicions concerning my pre-war Communist connections. Had I been compromised? I was able to reassure him on that score. For my part, I was particularly anxious to have Henry's reactions to the Molotov-Ribbentrop Pact which had placed me in a most unenviable position. After some desultory conversation, I plucked up courage and asked what the Russian interpretation was, expecting that the blame would be placed squarely on Chamberlain's shoulders. This was a delicate matter, for now that Russia and Germany were collaborating, I would not be prepared to cooperate with an ally of Britain's enemy. It was understandable that Henry was not anxious to embark upon anything resembling a frank discussion, but I was taken aback when he trotted out the old chestnut about dialectical materialism.

Our conversation fortunately came more down to earth and Henry tackled the concrete subject of our 'professional relations'. To my great relief, he proposed that I should not bring him any papers, thus sparing me the need to take a definite stand. So, during the first year of the Pact I was never asked for information. I did not, in any case, have access to secret data in the Treasury, unless the construction of new Post Offices could be regarded as confidential.

With Henry, my relations were correct but not cordial. I never had any cosy chats or meals with him (or with any other KGB agent), nor did I fix any appointments over the telephone. And I never heard a syllable from him about the existence of any other agents. In fact I can remember very few remarks of his which could be termed personal. The only information I ever obtained from him was that he was never allowed to attend Soviet films. However, he took that disappointment in a philosophical spirit, and on one occasion soon after his return to London, when no doubt I had also disappointed him about one thing or another, he remarked that I had enjoyed a good rest from his people. Henry never tackled any political issues, as Otto had on occasion, and I remember only one significant political comment, when he described Churchill as 'a crazy romantic'. Certainly his advice to me was on the standard lines: I was never to be seen to be living above my income, a stricture that was not in the least difficult, since even living modestly I had almost always a struggle to make ends meet. He warned that I had to keep a low profile in every way and when, for instance, I was asked by a research agency (PEP) to collaborate with Conservative MP Sir Richard Law on a piece on foreign policy (in which my name would not have appeared), Henry told me prudently to keep out. He also insisted that I should always speak of Communism in the sharpest terms. He did, however, apply a kind of etiquette to our relationship, even if this was largely a question of terminology, for he objected to the use of the word 'agent', preferring that of 'underground comrade'.

Even if I was always punctual at these routine rendezvous, I was hardly a model agent. On one occasion, I skipped an appointment in order to accept an invitation from a young lady to hear the opera *Carmen* at Covent Garden. Henry, pertinacious as always, rang up my flat and found out from a guest staying with me where I was spending the evening. He then made sure of intercepting me after the performance, when I had perforce to abandon the lady precipitously and ungallantly. There were also less bureaucratic moments, when he urged me to have an affair with an older woman whom, he believed, worked in a secret agency; and when I asked him for help when I feared (wrongly as it turned out) that a girlfriend was in trouble. Both proposals were rejected! On one occasion, when I reported that some holiday plans of mine had not matured, he even dished up a Russian proverb: 'One cannot jump higher than one's member,' he remarked in his own language.

My contact with Henry during the Molotov-Ribbentrop Pact was nominal and our infrequent meetings were merely a formality. I passed no documents to him, nor did he expect anything from me, and we never discussed the situation. Had the Pact continued to operate I would have broken with the KGB, whatever the consequences, but for the moment I was in no-man's-land.

After that disheartening winter of 1939 it was pleasant to leave London for a holiday in the south of France, which I did at the end of April 1940. Though fully mobilised, France still welcomed visitors although they had to obtain a visa in advance. By mid-May I was walking along the last few miles of a thyme-scented road to Les Baux, the capital of a medieval Provençal Lordship which gave its name to the mineral mined there known as bauxite. I spent an idyllic ten days at an excellent half-empty small hotel, and fully expected to stay for another week when news came of the German attack. Launched out of the blue through the Ardennes, the German army turned the Maginot Line and headed for the channel ports. I had no overwhelming urge to return to London but, fortunately for me, a beautiful French lady who worked in London for the French government and who was also staying at the hotel, decided to leave at once. I felt that her company on the journey back to Paris would make for a pleasant time, and we had no trouble reaching the capital.

There I discovered that to obtain a passage back to England I had to be issued with a ticket by the British Embassy in order to be guaranteed a place on the cross-channel steamer. At the Embassy I found the staff, including Donald Maclean, burning the records and I was roped in to help with the good work, so I took my turn with the load – wheelbarrow after wheelbarrow! This diplomatic precaution was more than justified, for disaster was in the air. Through her influential contacts in the French government, my friend was able to tell me that French resistance was breaking down and the Germans could not be stopped. All traffic was leaving Paris and making for the south, all taxis were commandeered by the military and there were dead lying everywhere along the roads. We took a train crowded with British refugees from Belgium and Holland to Boulogne, and went aboard ship as the German army approached Calais. We spent the night on deck in the thinnest of summer clothes, hourly expecting to be torpedoed, but we arrived safely in England around 20 May. In London the atmosphere was sombre, but there was no panic. Churchill had taken over from Chamberlain the day France had been invaded, and he soon created a mood of desperate resistance. It had been assumed that France would hold the western front while Britain would re-arm. With Britain's lack of armament and of the industry essential for war it would be an uphill struggle.

My work at the Treasury had been good training and it ultimately bore fruit for, as 1940 drew to a close, after two years of toiling on uninteresting if formative work, I was appointed Private Secretary to a Cabinet Minister and was brought into touch with the inner circles of the British Government.

SIX

Life with Lord Hankey

There was nothing surprising about my new appointment since it was customary for an Assistant Principal – the bottom rung in the hierarchy of the élite Civil Service – to spend a couple of years as Private Secretary to a Minister or a Head of Department. My new master, Lord Hankey, had the purely nominal title of Chancellor of the Duchy of Lancaster, but was in reality a Minister without Portfolio. Starting in the Royal Marines, where he had risen to the rank of Colonel, he had become Secretary to the Cabinet, and also to the General Staff, and Clerk to the Privy Council. After retirement from the Civil Service, he had been snapped up by Chamberlain, on the outbreak of hostilities, as a member of the inner War Cabinet. This had been the summit of Hankey's career, part of his eminence being due to sheer length of service in the mazes of Whitehall; but he was also highly regarded for his quiet and modest manner and for his ability in military matters, since he was almost alone in the War Cabinet in having the experience needed to stand up to Churchill in this field. Under Chamberlain, he had been a power in the land, known as a 'man of many secrets', but once Churchill took over as Prime Minister, Hankey's days of glory faded, and by the time I joined his staff he had been ousted from the War Cabinet, but not from the full Cabinet. As a Cabinet Minister, Hankey's main job was to direct a number of committees served by the Cabinet Office, the most important of which was the Scientific Advisory Committee (SAC) whose functions included the study of the scientific problems inherent in the construction of the atomic bomb.

One of Hankey's characteristics was his strong feeling for family ties, which was probably why he had chosen his son Christopher to work for him in his office. But even though under this arrangement Hankey paid his son's salary out of his own pocket, it was clearly unorthodox. Objections were raised, and Christopher was forced out. I was probably chosen as his replacement because I was on friendly terms with Hankey's other son Henry, whom I had known in the Foreign Office.

Hankey had been, and still was, a remarkable man. If we had been living in normal times of peace, I could not have asked for a more enriching and exciting job. It was just the right kind of organisation for me: it was small, friendly and intimate, conveniently situated in the Ministry of Agriculture building opposite Horseguards Parade, and within hailing distance of the Foreign Office, the Treasury and No. 10. The staff consisted of Lord Falmouth, a slim, distinguished peer who acted as the Minister's Scientific Adviser, and Sir Hugh Clement-Jones, a shipping magnate noted for his drafting skill, who was Hankey's general assistant. There were also two very competent secretaries and myself, and that was the lot. It was the most pleasant office I have ever worked in, and I have no doubt that, despite my basic disagreements on class structure, I would have been happy to stay with such a pleasant and important personality. Considerate, unassuming and cordial, he was so modest in his manner that he might have been mistaken for a City clerk. He occasionally invited me for a weekend at his country home where I saw what a happy family life he had. In the office he was equally gracious, and he had the unusual habit, for a Minister, of giving me personal advice from time to time. Although his tips, such as ensuring that one's notes always made it clear who took action or was responsible for taking action, might not appear extraordinary, they were all important. Of his gentleness I need only cite one instance: I had been guilty of excusing myself by saying 'pardon', which was then considered improper. Hankey gently corrected this to 'I beg your pardon', which is considered rather more correct in England. I felt impelled to say that the expression I had used was the usual parlance in Scotland and Hankey, to my astonishment, took back his remark. He also had a splendid sense of humour: I once had to compose replies to Christmas cards, and to one writer from what was then a colony, I drafted a reply which hoped that he would end up by rising to great heights; alas, I did not know that the gentleman in question was the Prime Minister of the colony. Hankey roared with laughter over my blunder.

It was also fun to meet people who had so far only existed for me in books or newspapers: Harold Macmillan, a future Prime Minister; Professor Chaim Weizmann, a founder of Zionism; and Oliver Franks who became our Ambassador in Washington in 1948. A pleasantly urbane figure, bulging with ability, Franks had a pretty turn of wit, which he applied even to such minor figures as me. On one occasion, when he and some colleagues were waiting for admittance to the ante-room, he quoted scripture at me under the flattering assumption that I was the guardian of the ministerial fort: 'Where two or three are gathered together . . .' Fortunately, I was familiar with the quotation, and indeed the lord was soon in the midst of them.

Hankey made no secret of his feelings about Churchill, both as to the Prime Minister's methods and especially his attitude to Russia. He also repeated complaints from his old military friends about the Prime Minister's habit of calling meetings late in the evening, when all those summoned were exhausted after a full day's work. The result, he alleged, was that many bad decisions were made, which afterwards had to be unscrambled. However, I never heard him criticise Chamberlain. On the contrary, he fully endorsed Chamberlain's policy of appease-ment towards Germany, and approved of the surrender at Munich in September 1938, comparing that agreement to the device adopted by Melanion (Hippomenes) of dropping golden apples when engaged in a race against Atalanta: by being tempted to stop and pick up the treasures, she had ensured her suitor's victory. (His analogy was completely fallacious, for the only result of Munich was to dismantle the fortified boundaries of Czechoslovakia, and part with a force equal to some six armoured and forty infantry divisions, as well as with a first-rate armaments industry. It was the equivalent of losing a major battle.) Yet the same man could see the folly of one-sided British disarmament, which forced Britain to reduce its defences below the safety level, and he exposed the weakness of numerous military policies by applying basic common sense. Again on the negative side, however, he seemed to have no idea of the country's fundamental industrial weakness, a disadvantage that became glaringly visible as the war progressed: inevitably the Government was forced to spend scarce foreign exchange currency on a host of elementary items from neutral countries such as

Switzerland. On the human resources level, he was quite blind to the defects of the public school system, which may have produced good officer material, but acted as a terrifying disincentive to inventiveness, technology, industry and commerce.

On the other hand, his judgements on other distinguished figures were sharp. He criticised the English style of his successor as Secretary to the Cabinet, Sir Edward (later Lord) Bridges, and dismissed Anthony Eden as a lightweight. He never criticised Leslie Hore-Belisha, the Minister for War, but his son Christopher was fiercely hostile to him.

Hankey's real ability lay in running the various Cabinet committees with tact and efficiency. Among these was the one that combed the radio industry for technicians to help in the rapidly developing radar industry. He presided, too, over a committee which assigned arms to Britain's allies, an exacting task which inevitably left a large number of discontented countries because there were never enough arms to meet the demand. The body which attracted the greatest attention, however, was the SAC with its defence panel responsible for problems concerned with the theory of the atomic bomb. Here, a pleasant atmosphere prevailed between Hankey and his committee secretaries in the Cabinet Office. These were all hand-picked and subsequently rose to great heights in later years. There was, for example, Group Captain (Sir) William Elliot who later became an Air Marshal, while Dennis Rickett was appointed to be a Vice-President in the International Monetary Fund. I was never secretary of that Committee, which is a Cabinet Office post, and my work on the atomic question was confined to a strictly administrative support role, trying to obtain passages on the heavily overbooked transatlantic planes for American atomic specialists. SAC also dealt with numerous other issues, such as liaison with the Dominions over photographic data, and it handled any questions the public might raise. One of the many bright ideas received was that of producing vitamin B from vegetable sources, which seemed to me to yield a product of much the same type as Marmite. Another rather more ambitious proposal suggested an ingenious method of deploying the Oerlikon anti-aircraft gun, a weapon sadly lacking in Britain. This idea was referred to Lord Falmouth, who rejected it with the inane comment that 'the sky is a big place'. Hankey fortunately read the reply before it went out, and referred the suggestion to the Air Ministry. He was often consulted by private experts on a wide variety of subjects, including air photography, and I remember his receiving an engineer who wanted to discuss defects in tanks. This was a common complaint, and the opinions of most soldiers on the vehicles supplied to them were usually unprintable. The engineer was unknown to him and came unrecommended, so Hankey fully expected him to be a crank or a professional carper. Accordingly, he instructed me to interrupt the meeting on some pretext after half an hour. When I faithfully obeyed these instructions, I was roundly snubbed and ordered to disappear. Clearly the visitor knew precisely what he was talking about.

Hankey was effectively the Minister for Science and he gave a memorable speech in the House of Lords about the different ministries and organisations in which scientific functions were carried out. I recall that when a Government committee was appointed to consider the conditions and remuneration of scientists in the various departments, the Committee's report was submitted to Hankey for presentation to the Cabinet. He asked me to prepare a draft and I was flattered that he adopted my text without changing a comma, and the document was approved by the Cabinet despite Treasury opposition to the extra cost. In fact, I myself found that the proposals did not go far enough, for they were only a first step towards tackling the age-old British prejudice against the technician and the scientist.

The essence of my work with Hankey, however, was at a rather more humble level. It was to ensure that correspondence was dealt with and, where necessary, filed. Sometimes Hankey sent communications of a more personal nature direct to the recipient, without passing through official channels, so I had no knowledge of them. Thus, on one memorable occasion, he wrote a letter to the Prime Minister, not entered on the files, protesting at the decision to curtail the distribution of confidential documents. Hankey presumably made the point that, to run his various committees, he needed to have a comprehensive picture of government activities and policies. Churchill was too busy to reply directly to all his ministers – that was the job of his Private Secretary who was then Roger Makins (later Lord Sherfield). I only learned of this because Makins sent me a positive reply, asking me to inform Hankey accordingly, which I did. Another time, he wrote a sealed personal letter direct to Churchill suggesting various concessions which we might extract now that 'these ruffians' (the Russians) had been attacked by the

Germans. But letters such as this did not form part of Hankey's ministerial duties, even though they have survived in his archives.

My post as Private Secretary brought with it an allowance equal to about half my salary, which was very welcome, since the Civil Service salary for beginners was so low. I therefore decided, for safety from bombing and air-raids, to move to a modern flat in Dolphin Square, overlooking the Thames. Dolphin Square was something of an innovation in conservative London. There was a certain aura of freedom from strait-laced society. I remember a skit at the Gate Theatre in which an innocent maiden was about to be seduced and murmured, 'O Dolly this is folly', while the shy young man uttered, 'O Rupert this is stupid'. He is finally assaulted by an entertaining lady who drives home her appeal with the cry that 'this is Dolphin Square where women are desperate'. It was not often my luck to run into such cases of despair.

I had hardly settled in when the building, which was supposed to be bomb-proof, suffered a direct hit, and I was only saved from death by the sheer luck of that bomb hitting a girder and exploding upwards. Since I was spending a sleepless night thanks to a badly filled tooth, I heard the plane overhead, the bomb dropping, and the falling debris in the room next door. When I looked around, there were no walls, but the staircase was sound, and I climbed down the four floors to safety wrapped in a blanket. Shortly afterwards, I was sleeping at my brother's house nearby when a bomb hit the neighbouring house. We all spent the night in the open, and this was unfortunately at a time when my sister-in-law was expecting her first child, Frances. This of course was the nightly lot of Londoners during the Blitz, but in such things I have always been lucky.

Unfortunately, all my new-found advantages seemed largely nullified by my uncomfortable position with the KGB. In May 1941, just before Germany invaded Russia, Henry made an exceptional request even though it was still the 'closed season' of the Molotov-Ribbentrop Pact, and I was faced for the first time with the problem of giving him information. Henry was worried that there was still a chance of Churchill compromising with Hitler. There was, in my judgement, no longer a possibility of a deal between Britain and Germany, but the need to reassure the Russians on this point was clear, and any confirmation of Churchill's steadfastness would help stiffen Russian resolve. Accordingly, I felt justified in taking soundings on this and on the crucial matter of possible negotiations between Britain and Germany for a separate peace – a consideration of the very highest priority to Russia, virtually an obsession. Ever since Munich, the Soviets had regarded Britain as a 'rotten plank' and their distrust had been compounded by the 1939 negotiations in Moscow for which they placed the blame solidly on Chamberlain. They realised that Churchill was a different kettle of fish, but they were still on their guard: there had been the notorious Venlo incident on the Dutch frontier with Germany in November 1939 when, by a clever piece of bluff, officers of the *Sicherheitsdienst* (the Nazi Security Service) had posed as opposition generals and abducted two British SIS officers. There were suspicions in Moscow that the Venlo incident involved the Germans trying to secure a separate peace with Britain.

The KGB's continued interest in the question of a separate peace became more intense after Rudolf Hess's solo flight to Scotland in May 1941 to contact the Duke of Hamilton and place before him a plan for peace. It has been alleged that certain homosexuals in British Intelligence lured Hess, the leader of Hitler's Nazi Party, into his escapade by exaggerating the strength of the peace faction in Britain, using the Duke of Hamilton's name in the process, but without the Duke's knowledge. I was pressed by Henry to provide information on Hess's flight, since the Russians were keen to get an exact picture of these extremely delicate overtures. I had no knowledge of the affair apart from what I had read in the newspapers, and told him so. (It appears from later revelations that the KGB obtained the information it required from Philby, thanks to a diplomatic contact of his.) Henry was disappointed also because I had not heard about Churchill's flight to Canada in a bomber to see Roosevelt. 'We must have been the only two people in London not to know about this,' he remarked bitterly.

When Russia was attacked by Germany in June 1941, I finally passed to Henry some documents of direct interest to Russia. I had no difficulty in having access to the secret papers in Hankey's office since I kept the registry. But I had to be careful as the office closed at 5.30 pm. and I sometimes had to stay on after normal hours. I was obliged to assemble the papers quickly, since I did not want to arouse the suspicions of the staff. I was therefore not always entirely sure that I had picked out just those documents I had in mind, and could never check them because in the morning they had to be replaced very quickly. My two main sources were Foreign Office telegrams and the Cabinet minutes, which were of a very general nature. The former were being obtained by the KGB from other sources; and the Cabinet minutes were stripped of any significant gems, the reader being referred to the more complete confidential minutes retained in the Cabinet Office where all delicate information was kept in separate files open only to a special few.

The Cabinet Committee papers, with the sole exception of the theoretical discussions on the atomic bomb, would have been of little interest to the Soviets; although there was some discussion in a few of the Foreign Office telegrams which I felt could confirm to the Russians the sincerity of Britain's declared intention to collaborate to the full in the common struggle against the Nazis. The only items I specifically remember concerned a method of defusing magnetic mines, which were taking a heavy toll of Allied shipping, and a memorandum showing that Britain was allotting to Russia a very high proportion of its arms assigned to Allies. No British secret information was included in any of these papers and I was not surprised at Henry's evident indifference to my material.

My association with Henry during this period consisted of brief evening meetings, usually monthly although sometimes fortnightly, often at an underground station near the Great West Road. I would prepare an envelope with the papers which I thought relevant, deliver them to Henry and arrange a rendezvous for their retrieval the next morning. Sometimes the transmission was in a public lavatory and usually there was never any problem, but on one occasion the hand-over was noticed by fellow users and I was surprised that the security-conscious Henry proceeded with the operation. Fortunately everything went off smoothly. At any rate, although I was often rushed I was never reproached by Henry for submitting confused or incoherent material, and to the best of my recollection he never made any specific requests as to what I should provide. He once offered me a small Minox camera, which would have had the advantage of reducing the two meetings needed for each hand-over to one, and I was given hasty instructions on how to use it by one of Henry's colleagues in the back of a car as we raced through London, constantly changing direction to evade surveillance. However, when I tried to operate the delicate apparatus at home, I rapidly rendered it unusable, not being gifted in mechanical matters, and the whole experiment was dropped.

Junior civil servants, originally excluded from mobilisation, were now about to be conscripted, so I anticipated that by June 1942 I would be swallowed up by the army and could forget about the KGB. I had hoped to ease out of my relationship with the Soviets at the earliest opportunity. The danger of invasion had almost disappeared by September 1940, when the Battle of Britain had been won. Pending my departure for the military, I bided my time patiently until I was called up to the Royal Armoured Corps in the summer. And so one of my most interesting periods in the Civil Service ended, and I made ready to face whatever the army had in store for me.

SEVEN

ENIGMA:
The Deadly Secret

My fate, I soon learned, was that my service in the armed forces would not be as a humble infantryman in the trenches; my next assignment took me into the heart of the war effort. I was posted to the secret and vital operation of deciphering signals of foreign military forces carried out at the Government Code & Cipher School (GC&CS), which had moved shortly before the war from the SIS headquarters in London to the small town of Bletchley, some sixty miles on the main railway line to the north, where it was safely hidden from German bombers. The school itself would not have aroused suspicion, set in the grounds of a hideous nineteenth-century Victorian mansion, which would serve as its administrative headquarters. But if one looked through the high steel fence which guarded the compound from intruders, one could see a cluster of dingy prefabricated huts of the type normally found in army camps. It was in these unimpressive structures that the most important technical breakthrough of the Second World War took place: the cracking of the ENIGMA cipher machine, a model of which had been provided to the British by a courageous group of Polish cryptographers who had been working for the Germans. Yet the final breakthrough was due to the skill and tenacity of British experts.

The staff at Bletchley Park, but mainly its cryptographers and other technicians, was a mixed group, chaotically assembled during the early years of the war. They were not the typical product of the older universities, where the cult and cultivation of social polish and homogeneity were mostly prized above scientific and commercial ingenuity. Churchill himself made the point with his usual pungent humour, in a rapid visit to the GC&CS in 1941, when he commented to Commander (Sir) Edward Travis, the Director: 'I know I told you to leave no stone unturned to find the necessary staff, but I didn't mean you to take me literally.' But these were the experts who produced solutions of genius for the nation's wartime problems by developing an even more ingenious device than the ENIGMA machine itself. This machine, designed by the mathematical genius Alan Turing, was a forerunner of the modern computer and reduced the laborious process of examining the infinite possibilities of interpretation to manageable proportions. The culmination of these efforts was that the unintelligible texts transmitted by the Germans in cipher could be 'unscrambled' and restored to their original text. This was not a once and for all battle, but a struggle to meet a constant challenge, since it was possible for the settings of the ENIGMA machine to be endlessly changed by the Germans; but the British technicians rose to the challenge. (We linguists only rarely caught a glimpse of the difficulties encountered by the technical side in the decipherment of the signals, which called for a different sort of mind.)

The linguists were more typical of an Oxbridge educational background and were later recruited in greater numbers in order to process the fruit of the progress made by the technicians. As fluency in German was a very scarce commodity in England, I was automatically assigned to ENIGMA when I was called up. I suppose my position as Private Secretary to Lord Hankey had been a sufficient guarantee of reliability, and I was taken on by the GC&CS and not even subjected to any interrogation.

After a short training in simple (non-machine) codes at nearby Bedford, which never proved useful, I was sent to Bletchley and put to work. We lived a semi-monastic life, which was only broken by the occasional visit to London to recuperate. There was a direct train to London, so that travel back to my flat there on my day off was not a problem. I had no car at the time and indeed not even a driving licence, but GC&CS was within walking distance of the railway station. Weekends were unheard of since the operational work was non-stop. Social functions too were virtually ruled out by working conditions and there were no common rooms. The rigid separation of the different units made contact with other staff members almost impossible, so I never got to know anyone apart from my direct operational colleagues. We did eight fully-occupied hours of work and then were transported back to our respective lodgings with families in the surrounding villages. Even within my hut, I never met some of the more important personalities, such as Peter Calvocoressi, who wrote a book on his experiences at Bletchley. Except for the work and the routine, I remember very little of what happened there during my twelve months' service. My territory was limited to my hut and to the functional and austere cafeteria, which could hardly be described as having a relaxed and inviting atmosphere.

When I discovered the nature of the work I was to be engaged in, I was proud to take part in this superb achievement of British brains, and was soon fascinated with the job itself. Few of us were military experts or had any knowledge of the details of the fighting, so our satisfaction was with the work itself. I found the editing of the German decrypts much like solving a crossword puzzle, or amending a corrupt text of a classical writer such as Molière. My work involved the correction and restoration of words blurred, distorted or omitted. This was a task which needed a generous dose of imagination, and a corkscrew mind.

The translators/editors operated in groups of six, including a team leader. The German ENIGMA (ULTRA SECRET) decrypts came in rolls of paper three or four feet long, each roll containing some ten signals. The leader's task was to decide whether the signals were worth processing (as was rarely the case), to check out if translations were accurate, and to make sure that no information was overlooked which had a tactical or organisational significance. For instance, at the beginning of my new career, I overlooked the implications of a particular phrase containing a reference to a German *Luftwaffe* unit in Yugoslavia, which could have been identified by relating this passage to a previous signal received two days earlier. There was another instance later on in which a passage did not seem to make sense, no matter how hard I racked my brains trying out various solutions. It turned out that two signals had been run together, and that this crucial factor had been overlooked by the expert attached to the cryptographic section.

The team leader had to ascribe a fictitious source for each signal and ensure that it was plausible, for the translation was careful never to give the slightest hint of the real origin of the document. The kind of source ascribed, for example, would be a mythical British agent such as an officer in the German Army High Command (OKW). Our product was known as the 'sanitised' version of ULTRA SECRET and was the one supplied to all recipients, including the War Office. (Recently some of these texts have been transferred to the Public Record Office, while almost all the German originals were destroyed, probably because Churchill hoped that the cracking of ENIGMA would never be made public.)

The work in Hut 6 was exacting, and traffic was heavy, but it was also varied. Sometimes, there were references in the deciphered messages to major German operations such as 'Sea Lion', the planned invasion of Britain in 1940, or 'the Final Solution', the elimination of the Jews by the Nazis. ENIGMA could have been a good source of information about certain aspects of the Holocaust, but it was not used for reasons of security, and there was a marked reluctance to touch on this explosive subject which had been known since 1941. Another message gave an insight into the psychology and methods of the enemy. It carried a severe rebuke from General Albrecht Kesselring, the German Commander-in-Chief in Italy, to his air squadrons for omitting to disperse their aircraft, which accordingly suffered serious losses in an Allied bombing raid. Occasionally even private messages were smuggled into the military traffic. I worked diligently on a letter from a woman officer stationed in Yugoslavia before realising that she was reporting that she had not yet found the right boyfriend, but lived in hope.

The German cryptographers kept the British constantly on their toes by introducing new techniques to baffle us. I remember the appearance of what we suspected was a new version of ENIGMA, which we knew as FISH and which the Germans called *Geheimschreiber*, or secret writer. I specialised in this new material but, from my point of view, the distinction was a technical one and only perceptible to the cryptographers.

My team leader, a regular army officer, was one of the finest men I ever met, and, thanks to his skilful and kindly guidance, tension was conspicuously absent. Harmony was stimulated by an adolescent jocularity which recalled college days. Our motto was: 'If you have not recovered on your *Abtag* [dog German for "day off"], you have only yourself to blame.' One memorable day General Stewart Menzies, Chief of the SIS (Secret Intelligence Service) who was known as 'C' and was in overall charge of ULTRA, passed hurriedly through the offices to survey his domain, and we had a visit from my old Treasury colleague, Claude Wilcox, charged with the task of seeing whether the

Government was getting its money's worth. He was artlessly shown a signal from General Rommel announcing a planned attack on the North African front, and was duly impressed.

I had been greeted on my first day at Bletchley by the receiving officer who explained to me the billeting system and informed me about other practical matters such as transportation to and from work. He emphasised the utterly secret nature of the decipherment operations and the need for complete secrecy in all our work, since, if the Germans suspected that Britain was reading ENIGMA, they would change the cipher and we would take a long time, if ever, to break into it again. We might even lose the war as a result. He ended the interview with the striking, if casual, announcement that we had not confided our ENIGMA triumph to the Russians 'because we do not trust them'. They were, he implied, a security risk.

This offhand announcement shook me and set my mind racing. I had arrived at Bletchley with the determination to sever my connection with the KGB. I felt certain that the Government, and Churchill in particular, would not have excluded the Russians from this important source of intelligence without the most cogent reasons, for the Prime Minister was known to be eager to assist the Russian ally in every possible way. I was therefore not ready to continue supplying them with material, even though I now knew that it contained information on German military operations on the Russian front. I would simply tell Henry that the risk was too great, or dissimulate that I had no real access.

There were two most probable grounds for the ban. I speculated and feared that even if the Allies won the war, their basic differences would, in the not-too-far-distant future, lead to the parting of ways. Even now relations were far from perfect. I recall Churchill's Private Secretary, John Colville, telling me that his master had once confided in him that there was no limit to the deceptiveness of the Russians. The Molotov-Ribbentrop Pact may have been thrust aside for the moment, just as the long list of Stalin's horrors was tactfully overlooked, but they could not be extinguished or forgotten. The other consideration was a technical but vital one. The Germans might now or later crack the Russian military cipher, and in that case, since the Russians would be making the most of ENIGMA information in their traffic, the Germans would soon be aware that their own cipher had been read. But there was more. I could not even exclude the possibility that the Soviets might be receiving ENIGMA with a false indication of the source. I had learned on many occasions in Whitehall that secrecy was a vital weapon in war. Churchill was a great believer in any deception which would protect our secrets, and made ample use of what he was to call a 'bodyguard of lies'. Would he not consider it essential to limit knowledge of the dissemination of the secret to as few people as possible? The receiving officer might then either have been given misleading instructions, or been briefing new staff members in all good faith by telling them exactly what he had been told to say. Thus, it was not to be excluded that the Soviets might already be receiving some form of ENIGMA. In fact, as La Fontaine puts it, '*Rien n'est certain que la chose incertaine.*' (Nothing is certain but uncertainty.) In any case, it was clear to me that the main interest of Bletchley was in the North African front and this was just a year after Germany had attacked Russia! Although concentration on Africa was to some extent understandable – since the German offensive might have brought the enemy into the oil-rich Middle East, and Rommel and his troops had at one point almost arrived in sight of Cairo – the Russian situation held the key to the outcome of Allied operations in Europe. Until then we had been operating from our island base; a small force acting alone against the overwhelming Axis Alliance. The entry of Russia into the war on the Allied side had signified a radical change in the overall strategic situation.

After turning the question over in my mind, I decided to consult a knowledgeable team leader whom I did not know but who had heard of me while he worked for a short time in Whitehall. I asked him to lunch and, after some general small talk, put my problem to him, but he did not have the answers. He confirmed what I knew from my days with Lord Hankey, that there was anti-Russian feeling among some senior members of the army staff, but he did not think that the receiving officer was misinformed. As far as he knew, the Russians were not being given ULTRA. He did tell me, however, that the main reason for this decision was the fear that the Russian ciphers might be broken, and might thus in turn reveal that the German ENIGMA had been compromised.

During the next few days my feelings of confusion gave way to the conviction that, much as I longed to absolve myself from any trace of espionage even to an ally, my liberation in the present circumstances would be morally unjustifiable. As more and more of the German

ULTRA decrypts passed through my hands, I saw that the signals contained a vast amount of precise information which would be of the utmost use to the Soviet armed forces in their struggle against the powerful German army. They would provide advance information of German intentions from which it would be possible to plan appropriate counter-moves. The ULTRA decrypts on the *Luftwaffe* gave details of the strength, unit numbers and location of the enemy's airforce squadrons. Furthermore, this data was not just limited to the *Luftwaffe*, but was related to the army as well, for the cryptographers had just accomplished a remarkable breakthrough and had cracked the *Wehrmacht*'s ENIGMA keys. In fact, it was now possible, as the charts on the noticeboard showed, to build up a clear picture of both land and air German orders of battle.

But perhaps what stirred me most, and forced me to rethink my position, was the news that the Germans were continuing to drive ever deeper into the Russian heartland in the south. My concern, even so, was not only for our ally, who was suffering huge losses: if the Russians were forced further and further back, it seemed elementary to me that there was a danger of their being reduced to conducting a guerrilla or marginal war, or even of collapsing. In that event the Germans would be able to switch a large block of their forces either to the Italian or North African fronts, or, worse still, to launch them against Britain.

As against all this, I asked myself with trepidation whether I would not be embarking on an enterprise fraught not only with danger for myself, but also for the whole Allied war effort. Theoretically there might be another Russian mole at Bletchley, but I had to consider the possibility that I was the only one in GC&CS and, if anything went wrong, it would be my entire responsibility. However, I reasoned that even ULTRA given in a sanitised form was not without risk and, if the secret had not already leaked, there was no reason, short of an unforeseeable disaster, why it should be betrayed to the Germans through me, particularly as I had every intention of exercising proper security. I reckoned that had Churchill wanted to let the Russians have raw ENIGMA, my personal KGB connection would have been safer than any military channel the authorities might choose. Naturally I would have wished to have had an opportunity of serving the Allied cause by more legitimate means, but this was only a most agreeable fantasy as I did not see myself knocking on the Prime Minister's door in Downing

Street and offering my services. I was only a junior and unimportant civil servant and I acknowledged that I would have to assume the burden alone if I decided to pass ULTRA to the Russians. I knew that my decision would in the end involve a large element of faith, because I could not be sure that the information provided would get to the right quarter, be applicable to specific situations and be used properly. Yet it was imperative that I seize the moment or else be tormented in later years for having let the opportunity go by. As it turned out, however, the benefits were, even if only by a miracle, roughly proportionate to the risks that were run; and a great consolation is that the secret was never betrayed.

My decision was taken on the night before I was due to travel up to London on my day off, just over two weeks after my arrival at Bletchley. It was then that I was to see Henry for the first time since I started my new job, and I had an opportunity to make a final examination of my conscience during the night. I could not get as much sleep as usual and this was due not only to the fearful problems weighing on me, but also to the fact that, after finishing the evening shift, which lasted from 4 o'clock to midnight, I stayed on in the office and spent the night on the floor of an unoccupied room, in order to avoid an inconvenient trip back to my lodgings.

I concluded, as I lay awake, that the situation only really offered two interpretations. The first was that we were withholding ULTRA from the Soviets. In that case, the refusal to pass on any information was indefensible because, despite the risk of a cipher leak, we were still dependent for our safety on Russia holding out. Alternatively, we were letting our ally have data even if we were not giving complete texts and not revealing the source. But, as I had already concluded, the absence of any leakage suggested that all was still well. Indeed, the provision of full texts in the original German would prove to the perpetually suspicious Russians that we were not manipulating the material. I was aware that they had even rejected Churchill's warning, based I believed on ENIGMA, of the imminent German offensive in June 1941, as a cunning attempt to set the two nations against each other; and in a talk with the British Ambassador, Stalin had put the blame for this gaffe on the deceptiveness of double agents. But it was clear to me that I should only agree to hand over secret material to Henry if he gave me satisfactory assurances regarding security of transmission, both from London to

Moscow and within Russia itself.

My relations with the KGB, strangely enough, posed much less of a problem than my decision to hand over the ULTRA material to them. Contrary to many other agents' experiences of the KGB, I had never been pressed to aim at a particular post, nor was I ever threatened. I was not surprised at this since, however naïve this may appear, I was convinced that they relied on my cooperation. From playing an essentially passive role with that agency, I was now in a position to transmit to the Russians vital German military information affecting their own operations against our common enemy on the Eastern front. This would be quite different from giving them information about Britain, which I had been unwilling to do. Russia was now an ally engaging the bulk of the German armies, ultimately helping to drive the Nazi forces out of Europe. Our Soviet ally was hard-pressed in the autumn and winter of 1942 when the Germans seemed on the point of capturing Stalingrad, and badly needed accurate intelligence. I could now provide or withhold from Henry the precious information that was in my possession and I was therefore in a strong position. Besides, I was no longer the uncertain youth caught in a skilful trap as had happened in 1937. Nor was I any longer afraid that the KGB might make my former Communist associations known and thereby ruin what had been a promising career.

In effect, it was thus that I recruited myself as an independent and voluntary agent, using the KGB as a channel to the Russians. If I can be defined as a spy, it is only in this solitary case, and it was my contribution of ULTRA for a period of a year which, I contend, gave meaning to and justified my maintenance of what had begun as a tenuous and unwilling link. Therefore, when I met Henry I did not hand over any material before discussing with him the question of security. I explained where I was working, what I did and the dangers which the transmission of original ULTRA intercepts involved. Fortunately, he was well aware of the risk of broadcasting ENIGMA by radio and he assured me that ULTRA would always be sent from London to Moscow by courier, and would never be included in the texts of signals within Russia. These assurances relieved a good deal of my anxiety and confirmed my own personal knowledge of the almost maniacal Russian insistence on security. It was only then that I delivered my first ENIGMA envelope to him. However, although he appeared pleased by and interested in my news, he was characteristically reserved in his reactions, exhibiting no special signs of satisfaction. I concluded that, as my previous performance had been so lacklustre, he probably needed guidance from his superiors on how to handle me. This was the first occasion on which I really felt that my KGB activities were performing a useful service, but I was not disappointed by his response and discounted his reserve, confident that the reaction of the Soviet army and airforce would be very different. It was for them I was acting, and not for Henry and his colleagues. It would be for the Russian generals to fit these documents into the overall picture. Of course, I would also have preferred to know whether there were any other KGB agents in Bletchley, but I knew instinctively that I would never be given the answer.

It may have been difficult for me to arrive at the decision to hand the ENIGMA material to the Russians, but there was no problem about obtaining the German decrypts for they were left around on the floor after having been processed. I also added to these the collections of my translations into English, since they expanded the coverage. I concealed the documents in my trousers in order to pass them out of the grounds, where I was never subjected to a check. I then transferred them into my bag at the nearby railway station. After that, they were handed to Henry in an envelope at some spot in the suburbs of West London. I would meet him at the entrance to the tube station, follow him to the platform and get out of the train when he got off. I would then trail him to a quiet spot, where the envelope was handed over. We never, as had been the case for earlier types of material, held a second meeting the following morning for Henry to return the papers to me. There was no need to do so, since the texts were routinely destroyed by the office.

The only problem was that of fixing the times of our appointments. We had arranged that, if there was any difficulty, he should turn up at the same place and time the following day; if that failed, the appointment should be repeated at the same time and place seven days after the first appointment. Only on very rare occasions was I inconvenienced, and so I made a half-hearted attempt to secure permission to have my day off on the same day each week, on the pretext that I had a date with a girl in London, but my request was refused. I did not insist, since any determined attempt would have looked suspicious. For a time, this procedure continued without any special incident or comment from Henry. Then, towards the end of May 1943, he announced with a triumphant smile that the Russians had won a great air victory in which they had destroyed 600 aeroplanes. His superiors had been delighted with my information and had granted me a decoration. He even confessed that he dreamed of my decrypts.

I rarely had time to read the German signals carefully, even those which I edited, and I was hardly ever in a position to assess the importance of the messages or correlate them with the bare announcements in the newspapers or over the radio, let alone the precise use to which they could be put by the Russians. All I was sure of was that the information I was providing was relevant to the general struggle for the survival of Russia. I doubt whether I would ever have understood, even at that time, to what extent I had influenced the outcome of the Battle of Kursk, the last important German offensive on the Eastern front, had Chapman Pincher in 1981 not connected me with that operation in his book, *Their Trade is Treachery*. Pincher was able to make the revelation because of disclosures from Peter Wright, the MI5 officer who interrogated me in 1964. What I was able to piece together from studies published in the 1980s astounded me and enabled me to make a complete reassessment of the effects of my action in 1943.

The Kursk salient, in the middle of the Russian front, was the main German target in the operation codenamed CITADEL. In preparation, during the early summer of 1943, the Germans deployed every piece of armour they could lay their hands on, which amounted to 2,500 tanks and assault artillery. The battle itself was to be the largest tank battle in history, involving a total of 2.2 million troops, but Hitler delayed the attack for almost two months until the beginning of July, and thereby lost the trump card of surprise. When the attack was finally launched, the German High Command was obliged to withdraw some of its crucial armoured forces because of the Allied attack on Sicily, and consequently lost any hope of rolling up the Russian army in the centre of the front.

After certain initial successes, when the Russians remained on the defensive, the Germans were driven back by the Russian heavy artillery which was cunningly concealed and adroitly sited. By 22 July, the Germans had been soundly defeated. They had lost over 1000 aircraft, including some 600 destroyed on the ground during the initial Russian air strikes, and their armour was so badly mauled that it was incapable of participating in any future large-scale offensive. By 5 August, the important German-held bastion of Orel had been seized, thus removing a threat to Moscow, and three weeks later Kharkov also fell. By a curious chance I was in my flat twiddling the knobs of my wireless when I heard the Russian radio broadcast the triumphant announcement that an 'old Russian city' had been recaptured, and I hoped, all in all, that my erratic and unpredictable efforts might have had some concrete result.

Judging from what has been written about the Battle of Kursk, my contribution materially assisted the air strikes which preceded the main offensive. It was clear from Henry's reaction that the air victory was based on my information, and solely on that. The Russians were convinced that, in its German version, the ULTRA I supplied was genuine, giving the full details of German units and locations, thus enabling the Russians to pinpoint their targets and to take the enemy by surprise, at least in the first raids.

We now know that I was not the only source with access to ULTRA. The KGB received English-language versions, or sanitised ULTRA summaries, from Leo Long, as an MI 14 analyst, but, as he worked only on the *Wehrmacht*'s order of battle, his information was limited mainly to land forces. In addition, there was also, as I had suspected at the time, the official channel, for the British Government had been sending certain selected ULTRA summaries in English to the Soviet Military Intelligence Service (GRU) almost from the start of the German invasion. This material may also have included some details which were useful in planning the Kursk air attacks, but such material cannot have been as useful to the Russians as the full, original German texts.

If the Russian success in the first air strikes was mainly due to my intervention, the position is more complex for the subsequent battle itself. The official, inter-Allied communications channel certainly gave valuable intelligence on the German plans and we know, for example, that at the end of April the British gave the GRU advance warning of the main features of the German plans for their offensive against Kursk. But this intelligence was far more restricted and more general than mine, although it probably had a wider coverage, since I could never be sure that I had all the relevant signals. Long's material was almost certainly more useful for the land battle, although, like the GRU information, it was usually couched in more general terms than mine since he was dependent on ULTRA summaries and had no access to the original intercepts. ENIGMA intelligence in any case played a key role in the battle itself, but the precise manner and role of each of the three forms will only be known when, if ever, the KGB and GRU archives are opened to public scrutiny. It is far from clear whether the Russians reciprocated with the provision of intelligence from their own sources.

As against my satisfaction at having helped our Russian allies to win the battle of Kursk, there remains the assumption that I revealed to the Russians (and therefore perhaps to the Germans indirectly) the knowledge that the British had cracked the ENIGMA codes. This accusation is completely unsubstantiated. No doubt the transmission of the ULTRA material itself implies the betrayal of that vital secret, but there were hundreds of other channels that might have revealed its existence: this is quite apart from several other Russian agents, such as Leo Long, known to have had access to ULTRA. He and his mentor, Anthony Blunt, close to the top level of MI5, had been initiated into the secret, as had Kim Philby, who had tried unsuccessfully early in his career to enter GC&CS, probably at the KGB's prompting. But, regardless of the various agents upon whom they could draw, the KGB did not, as far as is known, ever compromise the ENIGMA secret.

In any case, no additional material would have been required to guess that the intelligence 'from a first-rate source' supplied by His Majesty's Government to the GRU was obtained from SIGINT (Signals Intelligence). Churchill himself was disposed to let the Russians have the actual ENIGMA (that is, to let them know that it was based on radio intercepts), but he was dissuaded by his security advisers, apparently on the grounds that the Germans were able to read certain Russian ciphers. This ability, it is rumoured, was thanks to British assistance, rendered when Finland (which pinned down fifteen Russian divisions during the war) was attacked by the Russians in 1940. (I had seen old Russian decrypts in unused cupboards on my arrival at Bletchley. These were probably signals from the Finno-Russian war over two years earlier when Britain had provided the Finns with help in that field – I learned this from an old Foreign Office dispatch in Hankey's office. In that dispatch Halifax, then Foreign Secretary, had reproached the Finnish ambassador with his country's pro-German attitude, and reminded him of the aid which Britain had given his country at the time of its invasion by Russia. But low-grade ciphers of everyday battles are a different matter from traffic which might include ENIGMA material since no great skill was needed to penetrate them.)

But there were dozens of other less reputable sources of a potential leak, and the British authorities at the highest level were ruthless in their drive to preserve security. It was rumoured that Churchill had even gone to the lengths of sacrificing certain British convoys rather than arouse suspicions of having special information on the movements of German U-boats. And when SIGINT was used in cases of dire necessity, the extremely efficient British Double-Cross system (XX) was brought into play to show that the leakage was due to a well-placed Allied agent. Yet these rigorous measures were not foolproof. Many military leaders made reckless use of ENIGMA information in order to add to their laurels. General Montgomery, the victor of El Alamein, was a serious offender in this connection and was hauled over the coals for his lavish use of ULTRA, and ordered by Churchill to be more careful in future. The extent of the General's imprudence can be measured by the fact that for a time Montgomery's opposite number, General Rommel, sensing something amiss, stopped sending his messages by telegram, thus drying up the flow of information from ENIGMA. This clash between Churchill, backed by his security advisers, and Montgomery was the subject of hot debate at Bletchley, and I happened to overhear an argument between Professor Norman (the German scholar and a prominent member of the Bletchley staff) and a colleague in which Norman remarked contemptuously that Montgomery was 'only a general' thus underscoring the point that great skill in military tactics is not always accompanied by an understanding of high policy.

However, if Montgomery had excessive recourse to ENIGMA, it was in a good cause. The same could not be said of certain other offenders: one of the most flagrant lapses in security was committed by General Gatehouse, who had also played an important part in the crucial battle of El Alamein. In a talk to the National Press Club in Washington DC, he revealed that the British had broken the German code. Fortunately, most of the American journalists did not grasp the significance of his blunder, but it was forwarded to London by Reuters. Prompt action at both ends resulted in the leak being suppressed, but Gatehouse's career was blighted, and he was retired at the early age of fifty-two. Imprudence of this gravity occurred with horrifying frequency. For

John and Gabi in Geneva
shortly before beginning
their new life in Rome, 1952.

In Geneva with Gabi's
parents.

John and Gabi in front of 'La Banca' at the foot of the Spanish steps in Rome, 1954.

Press pass for John Cairncross, journalist for the *Economist*.

N. 0195

Sig. CAIRNCROSS John
ECONOMIST
corrisp. OBSERVER
Londra.

Roma, li 24 GIU. 1954

FIRMA DEL TITOLARE

Il presente documento, regolato dalle disposizioni emanate dalla Presidenza del Consiglio dei Ministri di intesa con i Ministeri dell'Interno e della Difesa, serve quale lasciapassare in occasione di pubbliche manifestazioni civili, militari e di avvenimenti eccezionali.

Il titolare è tenuto ad uniformarsi alle disposizioni impartite dai funzionari preposti al mantenimento dell'ordine pubblico ed assume tutti i rischi per i danni che possano derivare da eventuali incidenti.

The author in Bangkok as Chief Editor with ECAFE in 1961.

(*Above*) John with his ECAFE team in Bangkok, 1962.

During a conference in Vietnam – while working at ECAFE in Bangkok.

(*Above and right*) John at the
Food and Agricultural
Organisation for the
United Nations, Rome,
1983.

Gayle Brinkerhoff in 1983, the year she met John Cairncross.

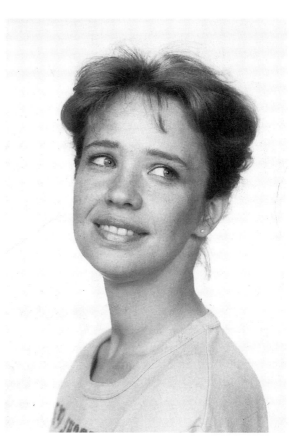

John, Gayle and their dogs in Rome, 1989 (© Fiorenzo Niccoli).

John and Gayle settle in the south of France at St. Antonin du Var in 1990 – before the storm breaks.

John taking a break from work on his autobiography.

John listening to P G Wodehouse while recovering from his first stroke, 1994.

The author returns to the UK after thirty years (Herefordshire, 1995).

The author at 'Longhope', west Herefordshire in August 1995 a month before his death.

instance, an Allied officer, though not entitled to knowledge of ENIGMA, was initiated into it, and even entered details in his diary which he carried into battle. Clearly, but for the unremitting watch kept by Stewart Menzies on the danger, the Germans would have soon learned that their most sensitive signals were being read by the Allies, with incalculable effects on the war effort. And so it seems that ENIGMA was safer in the hands of the security conscious Russians than in those of all-too-communicative Anglo-Saxons.

It may be asked, if in 1943 I realised that I was helping the military effort of the Russians, why I left Bletchley after spending only one year there. The answer lies partly in the shift system. There were three shifts every day for seven days a week, because the work was operational. The intercepts poured in continuously, so we were obliged to cover the flow without a break. Every week, one shift was moved on, from shift one to shift two, and so on. We thus had a slight bonus at the end of every week and it was badly needed, for this was an exhausting, if rational, arrangement. At the changeover of shift I would sometimes sleep from twelve to fifteen hours. I do not know whether any of my colleagues suffered as I did from the régime, and I heard of no such case, but I am very dependent on regular sleep, and large amounts of it. The continuous strain was telling on my health, the night shift proving an especially trying experience. In fact, the only high spots I recall in our limited social life were a concert of German Lieder sung by a colleague, and the Christmas pantomime where we were regaled by such items as a Russian partisan in a fur cap singing about his life, and revue items with cracks such as 'working and partly working' – courtesy of T.S. Eliot – and saving water by having baths 'à deux'.

There was a second reason for my leaving Bletchley. I might not have made an immediate attempt to secure a transfer had not Henry, at around that time, casually expressed an interest in my moving to Bletchley's Diplomatic Section, which was based in London and, as far as I knew, worked regular office hours. This seemed to me to suggest that the Russians were no longer concerned to keep me at Bletchley. As this fitted in well with my personal desires, I approached an acquaintance at the Foreign Office who had a particular responsibility for intelligence operations. This was 'Pen' Loxley, one of the most promising of the middle-level diplomats, later killed in an aeroplane accident. I sounded him out about the possibility of a transfer and he listened sympathetically, but replied, as I expected, that given the supreme military importance of the work at Bletchley, such a move was out of the question.

I then decided to explore other agencies to which I could offer my German skills. As luck would have it, I ran across Professor Frederick Green, a former French tutor at Cambridge, who in the modest rank of Captain was the liaison officer between Bletchley and Section V of SIS, which dealt with counter-espionage. He was a fellow Scot with much the same attitude to life as mine, and we got on splendidly. I explained my situation and, as Green was not on good terms with Travis, the head of GC&CS, he lent a sympathetic ear to my plea, based essentially on health grounds. Green was as good as his word and presented my case to SIS, emphasising that I had not only an excellent knowledge of German but, as I was flattered to hear, a keen intelligence. Green must have put his request very skilfully, but unfortunately Bletchley learned of my approach to Section V, and the affair became envenomed. Indeed, the situation deteriorated so badly that I was obliged, after receiving an assurance from Green that my application to SIS would be approved, to pull out of Bletchley altogether. Thus for a short time I was in a kind of vacuum and I spent a brief but somewhat disturbing few weeks unattached to any organisation.

I had not warned Henry of the possibility of such a move, and when I reported it to him, he was shocked, but exercised acute self-control and did not explode. I was amazed, for I had obviously taken a step that ran counter to all the KGB's rules. (Sometimes a *fait accompli* is the most effective retort.) Henry would have had to report to his boss, and there was nothing the KGB could do to me; but at our next meeting, he put the greatest pressure on me to go back to Bletchley, offering me £100 as an inducement, which I refused. I explained that such an idea was out of the question, and would destroy any reputation I had at Bletchley – or in intelligence quarters anywhere.

Henry's proposal that I move to the Diplomatic Section puzzled me, and my intuition now is that someone had blundered in this whole affair, for I am convinced that there were no other KGB sources in GC&CS. Henry must have misinterpreted a suggestion from his masters, otherwise his conduct in suggesting the move would have been inexplicable. He must also have informed Blunt, rather than admit his mistake, that there was someone else at Bletchley, explaining that his agency had others just as good as Cairncross. Finally Blunt must have accepted this bluff, and have passed on this version in his confession to MI5.

My eventual move from Bletchley to SIS at St Albans – as in all other cases – was made on my own initiative. By the autumn of 1943 the tide had turned in the war against Germany; and although getting away from the ultra secrets of GC&CS did not mean getting away from Henry, I would now be in a less sensitive position in a different organisation. I no longer wanted to be in a position of such importance to the KGB.

EIGHT

With Philby and Greene in the Secret Service

When I arrived at St Albans, my SIS security examination by Colonel Felix Cowgill, head of Section V, focused on the refugee *Luftwaffe* officer who, after a referral by me, had been brought to Britain with his fiancée by the Air Ministry because of its interest in the radar apparatus he claimed to have invented. Embarrassingly, it had proved to be of no interest and when war broke out he had been interned. 'Wilhelm' wrote to me asking me to intervene, but this I was quite unable to do and we lost contact. My explanation of this encounter seemed to satisfy Colonel Cowgill, and the only other question he asked was whether I was fit for military service, perhaps because he was being pressed to keep down the number of staff who might be better used in the fighting services. I told him that I was fit, and had indeed been called up in 1942. I was accepted none the less, my fluency in German tipping the scales in my favour.

My feelings were of immense relief, for there was no longer any danger of my being again assigned to shift work. I could live in my London flat and take the train to the office at St Albans. This meant getting up at six o'clock – and being awakened by the tick of my alarm clock just before it went off – but working regular office hours on an interesting job with agreeable colleagues in pleasant country surroundings soon did wonders for my health.

Section V of SIS was responsible for counter-espionage abroad, receiving military intelligence traffic from the *Abwehr*, the German Military Intelligence Service under Admiral Canaris. I was assigned to the *Sicherheitsdienst* (SD), the German counter-espionage unit. This formed part of the Reich's *Sicherheitshauptamt* in Berlin, whose six sections included the Criminal Police and the ill-famed *Gestapo*, or Secret State Police, as well as other functional divisions, such as one that dealt with political and related attitudes. The role and importance of the SD was expanding. This was because the *Abwehr*, and Canaris, were justifiably distrusted by Hitler, just as he was never sure of the *Wehrmacht*'s loyalty following its defeatist attitude in the days before the outbreak of war.

The *Abwehr*'s cipher, like the other ENIGMA keys, had been broken at Bletchley and texts were processed at both Bletchley and in Section V. We handled the German originals though these were gutted of any information on agents and then carefully indexed by, among others, a highly competent lady named Mami who was in charge. Efficient recording was central to effective counter-espionage, and the work of Section V paid off, almost all the *Abwehr*'s agents infiltrated into Britain being caught and 'turned' by MI5. The ease with which this was achieved was due to their skilful handling, but also reflects a weakness on the *Abwehr*'s part. It was hardly surprising, therefore, that the *Abwehr* was soon controlled by its rival, the SD, as the role of the Nazi Party increased in all fields of military activities. My work as an editor did not involve any contact with or research into SIS agents, but was confined to the analysis of general policy. There was a sharp division between the staff who catalogued and analysed the data on agents and those who edited text. I hate to disappoint those for whom the Secret Intelligence Service is peopled by 007s, but the reality was much better reflected by a cartoon in *Punch* as a crowd of small unimpressive bowler-hatted figures scurrying to their offices.

I had expected that the *Abwehr* signals might prove useful to the Russians, particularly as they did not directly involve British interests, but the information I eventually provided was received with complete indifference. Following the standard KGB policy, Henry did not tell me his reasons. (The mystery was solved when I later learned that Blunt was on MI5's circulation list for the *Abwehr* telegrams.)

The head of my German section was David Footman, who was always calm, balanced and equable, but the Chief disliked him. This was perhaps unavoidable, for there was a sharp contrast between his intellectual personality and 'C''s foxhunting and clubland background. Footman, however, was more vulnerable because of his friendship with Burgess than because of his personality and so, after Burgess's defection, Footman was eventually removed as part of the general clean-up that followed. I am sure that Footman found me rather awkward. On arrival from Bletchley I was still run down and on one or two occasions I found it difficult to get up in the morning. Footman, reasonably enough, insisted that I should have phoned the office to let them know that I was not coming in. However, the fact was that it was just as much of an effort for me to phone as to get up. If I could have phoned, I would have got up and gone in, but I did not offer this explanation, since I knew it would have made a bizarre impression.

The head of the Iberian branch of Section V was Kim Philby, and working for him was Graham Greene. Philby was widely regarded as an up-and-coming man and certainly had a very clear mind, writing memoranda which were always crisp and 'going somewhere'. His handwriting, readable and tidy, reflected a forceful mentality. His style, according to his right-hand man, Tim Milne, was similar to Stalin's, but I am not capable of judging the similarity. Despite the intense pressure under which he worked, he was always smiling, in good humour and seemingly indefatigable. (Later, after I had lived for a short time in the Indian sub-continent, I was struck by the similarity of his inner calm and the ability of so many Asians to remain unruffled in stressful circumstances. It was not for nothing that he had spent his boyhood in India.)

Philby was somewhat unconventional in his manners. I once asked him and another friend to lunch at the Travellers, and he turned up in his usual old green military jacket. He was dressed in just the same way at the only other meal I shared with him, which was with Lord Rothschild. The only remark I remember from this meeting, my presence at which arose from an error in my diary, was made by Rothschild who, on picking up the bill, said with a grin: 'Ten pounds. I'll have to claim this for sucking up to Kim.' The two men were clearly on the most friendly terms and I recall Rothschild giving a lecture to Section V, with Philby in the chair, on his own heroic work for MI5 on defusing explosive cargoes on British ships.

I never talked politics with Philby except to try out on him, once or twice, my theories about Nazism becoming more and more radical, with a growing opposition to the upper-class Establishment. Philby always sharply rejected these ideas, and I now think that this was because he was unwilling to accept any suggestion that Germany was moving towards a kind of Nazi Bolshevism. I may add here that I never knew whether he was in on my recruitment or not, and there is only one conversation of his which strikes me as revealing in retrospect. This was after I had returned to the Treasury at the end of the war and our conversation was about the ten-year prison sentence handed down to the atomic spy Allan Nunn May in May 1946. He asked me what I thought about it, and I replied that, in the circumstances, the sentence was inevitable. He went on to say that it had not been certain at the beginning whether the accused would plead guilty. When he did, 'the MI5 boys cheered up'. The case was not quite such an open-and-shut one as it seemed because the evidence in court had been derived from signals intelligence obtained from the Soviet defector Igor Gouzenko, and the authorities were probably not too happy to compromise this evidence in court.

As regards 'C', his role as chief of SIS had been sharply curtailed by the expanding value of SIGINT. It was no secret that, during the war, his continued importance was largely based on his insistence in securing total control of Bletchley. Naturally I had very little contact with 'C', who functioned at an infinitely higher level, with the rank of Minister. He was extremely adept in his efforts to control the circulation of ULTRA and his influence extended to all the services in their use of it. He was also very effective in inter-departmental meetings in Whitehall, and in the art of inter-office skirmishing. Thus, when there were complaints about the provision to the services of prompt and sufficient intelligence, he countered by offering to add to his office an official from each service who would be able to supply guidance on the type of information required. He was immediately furnished with three officers who, as could easily have been foreseen, were selected from among the weaker brethren. And so harmony prevailed, 'C''s personal reputation was enhanced, and that of his organisation preserved. The one occasion on which I came into contact with 'C' was when I was editing a report on conditions in Germany submitted 'by an engine driver in a neutral country'. This country could only have been Switzerland, for there were no railway communications between Sweden and Germany, and in the circumstances it seemed to me that there was no reason to suppress the source's Swiss origin. Indeed, I reasoned that, if revealed, it would give the report greater credibility or at least an air of reality. For my presumptuousness I was given a royal rocket by the Great Man.

I had not been working long at St Albans when the office moved back to London – a move inspired, it was said, by Philby. The importance of counter-espionage against Germany was rapidly diminishing. Section V was gradually switching its focus to Russia, as was reflected in the revival of another section to deal with that country. Philby, once he had engineered a putsch against Felix Cowgill and taken his place as head of Section V, annexed this new unit (Section IX) as soon as its head, Jack Curry, retired.

As peace approached and the war effort against Germany was run down, it was not surprising that the staff of my office was reduced, and my work lost any interest it might have had. However, some prospective employers within SIS began to look for new recruits and the Director of Section I (the political division) when on a visit to my office, made a suggestion about joining him, and offered me a transfer to the intelligence-gathering branch of the Political Information Unit which I accepted.

I was soon propositioned about staying on in SIS, which would no doubt have led to my being posted overseas as their representative, but it seemed to me that the intelligence officer abroad had the functionary's usual load of routine, producing results that were far from satisfying, and enjoying no very brilliant career prospects. Nor did I feel especially gifted for the task of running agents, which requires a special type of character and a temperament different from mine. I also had considerable doubts about the value of such work, as any wartime glamour in it had disappeared. There was, moreover, not the slightest reason for maintaining the KGB connection, the situation regarding Russia now being the reverse of what it had been when I was recruited, or when I had been working at Bletchley. Far from being even formally cordial with the Russians, our two nations had become deeply suspicious of each other. I realised that the Cold War was in the offing and I no longer considered I had anything to contribute to the Allied cause. I therefore got in touch with Harry Wilson Smith, the brilliant and pleasant Personnel Officer at the Treasury. I asked him if there was any chance of my being, as he put it, 'winkled out' of wartime service. My request was approved and I was soon installed in my old seat, where I was welcomed back by my former Treasury colleagues.

I had made few friends during my service with SIS, but one exception developed into a life-long friendship and became the one lasting recollection of my days at Section V. It began and ended – with the fittingness of fate – in a typical intelligence setting, and my first meeting with Graham Greene was original in every sense. It might have been lifted out of a novel. While travelling up and back every day to St Albans from London I would use the time to get some reading in. One morning as I was sitting in my train at St Pancras station, a tall lanky figure whom I recognised as a colleague of Kim Philby, stopped outside the carriage and asked if he might join me. I readily agreed, and after a few moments the newcomer sitting opposite me asked what I was reading. I told him that it was *England Made Me* and went on to say how much I was enjoying it, and how lucky I had been to pick it up, since wartime austerity rather restricted the range of books available. He nodded and said that in his opinion it was not a bad novel. I was encouraged to tell him that there were even better books by the same author, such as *The Power and the Glory*. 'Yes,' he agreed less cautiously while leaning back reflectively, 'it is a fine piece of work.' (Quite unwittingly, I had struck just the right note for, at our very last meeting, he said that this was his best effort, and what was even more interesting, was also his personal favourite.) Intrigued by what seemed a hint that he belonged to the writer's circle, I was bold enough to ask him if he knew Graham Greene. 'I am Graham Greene,' he replied, underplaying what was a veritable *coup de théâtre*. After that, we never turned back; and from that day on, he dubbed me 'Claymore' after the Highland broadsword, and this name has followed me throughout my life. In 1948, I even received a letter from Graham's secretary addressed to 'Mr Claymore? Esq.' – and now that Graham is gone, his delightful niece, Amanda, has spontaneously carried on the tradition.

Graham Greene was for me not just a superb writer, but a wonderful and loyal friend. I was originally surprised that he should have taken to me back in 1943, for he was already famous and I was not in any way distinguished. Our upbringing and background were also very different: he was a dissident Catholic, while I was an unbelieving Calvinist. But it took Graham's insight to bring out the contrast between my non-faith and his creed. We chanced to meet one evening in the foyer of the small Gate Theatre during the interval. I can still remember hearing the trains rumbling through the neighbouring underground station. As it happened, having lost a pivot tooth, I was on all fours calmly searching for it. I could see Graham looking on with surprise at my unruffled behaviour. But he astonished me when, with a look of sadness, he expressed his envy of the Calvinists who are always so confident, convinced as they are that they have been saved. Indeed, it was only at that moment that I realised how deeply my self-confidence went back to my Presbyterian upbringing.

This contrast, however important, masked a similarity in our approach to life which was at the root of our affinities. Not only were we dissidents, but we were unconventional characters who defied or ignored public opinion. I have never been a respecter of persons, but for Graham it was more a matter of rebelling against accepted wisdom. He even seemed to revel in his departure from the standard rules of decorum. Thus he would welcome the arrival of winter, when the candles had to be lit for dinner, emphatically preferring the beautiful yet artificial lighting to the natural rays of the sun. He also referred caustically to the 'noisy hens' who disturbed his quiet when in the countryside. Not for him the romantic love of rustic pleasures, which has been with us ever since Horace's ode about the businessman who talks, not quite sincerely, about the peasant's happy life.

Graham's rebelliousness, however, was far wider and deeper than this disregard for convention. It was pithily and uninhibitedly expressed in his 1969 speech at Hamburg University on the virtue of disloyalty which has stayed in my memory ever since I heard it. His attitude to religion is the obvious example of what has often been regarded as his contrariness. Catholic converts, at least in England, are noted for their unquestioning adherence to their faith. However, he was consistently critical of many of the Church's dignitaries, though it was usually clear to me that he made a distinction between operations which he referred to as religious politics and the faith itself. He made no bones about his dislike of Pope Paul II and he quoted ironically a phrase used by his lawyers in correspondence with the Vatican: 'with deep respect for the sacred purple'. In talking to a young priest, he referred slightingly, but typically, to a certain group of Catholics as 'the faithful', and it will be remembered that, in his works, priests are all too often portrayed as obtuse, insensitive and obsequious. The same unorthodoxy is carried over to the related question of sex interdicts. He was deeply convinced of the sinfulness of offences against the Church's sexual code. I once tried to interest him in the incomparable poetry of Dante by reading him the marvellous episode of Paolo and Francesca, ending in the unforgettable line, which tells us how they fall into each other's arms:

And in that book that day no further read.

But the one point which he found worthy of comment was the irrevocable damnation by which the ill-starred lovers paid for their sins.

Graham's various affairs have been fodder for innumerable mindless articles, and the contrast between religion and transgression certainly still strikes such ex-Protestants as myself, who are even more taken aback by the Catholic note which repeatedly emerges in his love life. In the incident at the Gate Theatre, Graham was accompanied by his lover Dorothy Glover, who in our subsequent conversation, dwelt enthusiastically on the rapid spread of Catholicism in England, which forced many new converts to wait patiently in line before they could be instructed in their new religion. His later lover Lady Walston, Graham told me, regarded herself as not married to her husband (since the two had not been joined by a priest), and he exulted in the fact that the children of this union were being brought up as Catholics. His thirty-year devotion to Yvonne, which was only ended by his death, and to which he always referred with pride and joy, was based on shared views which reflected the same tension between faith and morals.

He struck a curious note on the role of women when we discussed my book on Christian polygamy, *After Polygamy was Made A Sin* (1974), which he found amusing and penetrating, referring to it as 'the dirty book by Claymore'. He was particularly impressed by my remarks on Leyser, a seventeenth-century German enthusiast for plural marriage whom he praised as 'such a splendid fellow'. A mutual friend, Paul Riess, felt that Leyser's view of woman as intended almost exclusively for breeding purposes savoured a little of misogyny, but I never got a chance to ask Graham why he thought so highly of Leyser.

Throughout the years Graham followed my career with interest and attention, but we rarely talked of literature, for he was a well-rounded man rather than a *littérateur*. He would tell me of his new ideas, such as that of writing a novel about a Catholic who kills himself for the love of God, and we had desultory discussions about Shakespeare's chronology and why, to my dismay, he did not appreciate that exquisite and witty poet, La Fontaine. The only reason he ever gave me for this coolness was that the Fables were spoiled by the need to observe the rhymes. I did not feel obliged to explain that I had had to take considerable liberties as regards the rhyme in my translation (*La Fontaine Fables and other poems*: 1982), and that, had he been able to enjoy the poems in the original, he might have changed his view.

At our last meeting in Antibes, our conversation turned to his writing, and his remarks were, as always, illuminating. He told me of another book he was planning and there was certainly nothing of the agony and the ecstasy about his creativity. He said that, once he had hit on the central idea for a work, the rest simply flowed effortlessly out of him. This may be, to speculate, because his novels were not fabricated, and they came from a particularly rich and deep dimension. In several of his books, the subject of saintliness comes up. I am no expert in this field, but I do not think that I am going astray when I contend that he was far closer to sainthood, with all his erratic traits, than the austere but cardboard figures which are still served up to us as the genuine article.

In the field of Intelligence (as well as in business and in all practical matters generally), he seemed to me free from the anguish and tensions which he accepted where religion inspired or weighed on him. There was no sign of a constant rebellion against conventional standards. On the contrary, he showed a dispassionate and impressive sense of realism. It may be, of course, that the underlying analogies between the penetration of the secrets of the human mind and those of Intelligence are such that he was equally at ease in both fields. His passionate dislike of injustice and his sympathy for the underdog never distorted his judgement in threading his way through the treacherous maze of espionage and counter-intelligence. I felt that he was justified in his scathing remarks about the cocksureness of molehunters who fantasise without any experience of Intelligence. However, he may well have been influenced by his close association with Philby.

I never had any dealings with Graham in the SIS offices, and cannot therefore express any opinion about his work, but from my talks with him, I am certain that his understanding of intelligence operations was never blurred by the romanticism visible in the work of many other writers. Had Graham had any inclination to carve out a career for himself in Intelligence, he could, I am convinced, easily have done so. After Kim Philby's promotion to head of Section V of SIS, he worked under Tim Milne, and when Tim followed Kim up the ladder, the natural choice for a successor fell on Graham. He resisted the offer vigorously, for he had neither the need nor the desire for a new profession. In particular, he was never interested in power and finally succeeded in declining the appointment and securing it for his friend and colleague, Desmond Pakenham, a competent officer and a brilliant linguist. I thought they formed an excellent team inside and outside the office and I remember seeing them, after Section V had moved back to London, going merrily off together to a sex show in Soho.

NINE

Victory – But Not For Me

I had been an agent for the duration but the war was over, and while I reluctantly remained in contact with my controller Henry, it would surely be merely a matter of time before I would sever my connection with the Soviets.

I rejoined the Treasury in 1945, glad to feel that there could be a return to something approaching normal life after the struggle to win the war, and the privations endured even by civilians. The adjustment to peacetime conditions was, however, not easy and morale sagged as it was slowly realised that prospects for the future were not bright. Britain had emerged from six years of constant struggle exhausted, with a suffering economy and the nation's coffers empty. Industry was slow to adapt – its modernisation held up by gaps in British technical education and out-of-date equipment. To make matters worse, rationing was stepped up and shortages were even harder to bear for the struggle was no longer there to sustain us.

I visited Dutch friends in Holland some six months after VE day, and was impressed by the recovery of their small hardworking country which had been largely un-industrialised until the war and dependent on its agriculture and its Empire, now lost. I brought back from my holiday a bottle of eggnog (advokaat) which I kept in my office cupboard, and from which I took a sip from time to time to give me a short spurt of energy, for like practically everyone else, I was worn out by wartime strains. Britain had been fortunate in ensuring adequate food by having a competently managed rationing system supplemented by the help of generous American aid, and we never starved; but there was a national outburst when American supplies of dried egg powder were stopped on the assumption that Britain had returned to normal conditions. The system was fair, and free from corruption, although I remember my sisters protesting vigorously at the decision not to allow extra sugar for jam making. I also remember Churchill's intervention to allow exchanges of rationed foods between families. For people like myself, who relied on fruits and vegetables, and who lived alone and did not cook, the diet was dull and unsatisfying.

The Allied victory put me in a more difficult position than ever when Russia and the West began to fall out. Divergent interests and views were bound to pull them apart, especially given the Soviet conception of a protective glacis, which meant the imposition of a Communist régime in almost all of Eastern Europe. The confrontations were particularly acute in Greece and Italy where there were strong Communist Parties. On the other hand, the underground organisations set up with the help of Western governments to combat Communism often gave rise to movements which became outposts of the Fascists and assisted many war criminals to escape to safe havens in South America. I felt completely out of the political struggle, and I certainly had no wish to join the Stalinist empire; and I now almost regretted my earlier association with the KGB, which still seemed determined to keep me on as a kind of sleeping partner.

The Treasury after the war controlled expenditure by other departments and dealt with foreign finance. It recruited its administration from other departments after checking their records but its staff was chosen annually by examination. There were three main departments: Matériel, Personnel and Finance. To begin with I was posted to the Defence Matériel Division where one of my functions was to deal with surplus war disposals, which were the responsibility of the Ministry of Supply. The decisions to be taken were of a purely routine non-secret nature, the only delicate subject that came to my notice being the approval of the construction of a uranium enrichment plant. The decision, however, was taken at a higher level, and no notes explaining policy were attached to the paper. Files marked 'Secret' were practically non-existent, and even when one occasionally passed through my hands, I felt no obligation to transmit it to the KGB.

In 1947 I transferred to Defence Personnel, where my responsibilities were precise and simple and dealt mainly with proposals for the gradings and complements of senior officers in the Armed Forces. The main problem was how to reshape the forces to peacetime requirements,

"Their Lordships were somewhat taken aback"

H.M.W.

which had fallen sharply after demobilisation. One of the bonuses of this tedious assignment was that I had to visit the various Commands to inspect their work and discuss the position of the officers concerned. I was thus able to visit charming old cities such as Bath, Salisbury, Shrewsbury and York for the first time.

In London I would often run into Graham Greene and on my Treasury trips I never forgot to collect miniature bottles of whisky for him – some of which were turned to good account in the film of his novel *Our Man in Havana*. He was always grateful for these and wrote, 'I consider the Stratford-on-Avon whisky the sinister gem of the collection.' I had a marvellous evening with him in London when I was entertained by him together with a French novelist. We were first taken to see *The Rake's Progress* and ended up with a splendid late dinner at Rules. We also met at the Old Vic, where Laurence Olivier was acting in a Shakespeare play and was, Graham thought, 'jazzing up' his role. Then I met him again with a beautiful Australian girl, whom I had previously seen in the company of the philosopher Freddie Ayer.

I moved in 1948 to the Exchange Control Division where I was appointed Deputy Treasury Representative on the Western Union

Finance Committee, the only Treasury assignment which could be remotely considered sensitive. The Union was an alliance of the West European countries, including France and Portugal but not Spain. In a way a forerunner of NATO, it is still in existence and has indeed taken on a new lease of life representing an independent Europe in which France was more ready to participate than in NATO, where American influence is preponderant. My assistant was Robert (later Lord) Armstrong who was destined to become Secretary to the Cabinet under Mrs Thatcher. The Treasury Representative himself was a more senior officer for whom, as his assistant, I did the occasional odd job. His task consisted essentially of allotting Union expenditure on arms between its members, and no technical details were discussed. The budgetary calculations were complicated and the composition of a report sometimes had a talmudic complexity. When I started the job I had been told that the post would be upgraded, the sitting tenant clearly having a good claim to the next grade. As it turned out, although my reports were appreciated, I did not get on well with my boss, and a colleague was appointed instead. I still had hopes of promotion but I was again passed over, although my work was warmly praised, and it became clear that I must look elsewhere for job satisfaction.

Although I had felt that I ought at least to give the Treasury a further trial, I was having increasing doubts about my suitability for Civil Service work. A possible alternative was my original hope for an academic career, and I took soundings, but without success. My professor, Harry Ashton, gave me a glowing recommendation which I was unwise enough to send, in its original form, to a provincial university which promptly lost it; and I made a few approaches for junior posts elsewhere. I was strengthened in my inclination to move on by my involvement in the preparation of a book with my eldest brother, Andrew, on Shakespeare's business career: i.e. how much did he earn? It had been commissioned for inclusion in a French series, my brother undertaking the research and presentation while I would do an analysis of the role of money in Shakespeare's time, plus the translation. I was also still working on my book *New Light on Molière* which I had started at Cambridge. These efforts were, alas, incomplete, and since I had no previous experience and had not produced any published articles, my applications were refused.

I then had the idea that there would be more scope for enterprise in business, but I was advised that large firms were just as constraining as Ministries, and without the *esprit de corps* which is so often found in government work. Thanks to an introduction to a senior executive in Courtaulds, however, I was offered a post there and was about to take it when my Personnel Officer extracted the name of the firm from me, and at once blocked my move: for what reason I remain in ignorance.

My contact with the KGB during this time remained merely formal. No doubt they hoped that I would in time obtain access to more important information, although I was now busy organising my departure from the Civil Service. The kind of information I passed in those post-war years was relatively innocuous and only consisted, for example, of telling my controller how the Air Ministry was able to make deductions about a Russian aeroplane on the basis of the size of its wheels. The moment for me actually to sever my KGB connection never came, but sometimes one is forced into a move which one should have had the energy or the initiative to make of one's own accord: in short, my problem was solved by events.

There were two important events in 1951 which changed my life. I married an accomplished young German lady who had acquired British nationality in 1934, Gabriella Oppenheim, whom I had met in London. She had recently moved to California, for she had relatives and friends in the USA, but after some hesitation she decided to return to England and marry me. My mother, who knew each of her children well, remarked when she learned that I was going to marry a continental girl, 'You always wanted something different.' Only Peter (Yuri Modin, who became my controller in 1947) seemed somewhat shaken by the news. Gabi and I married in London at Kensington Register Office on 26 January.

It was also in the spring of 1951 that news of the defection of Maclean and Burgess hit England with gale force, causing a tremendous stir. Their famous flight to the Soviet Union in May verified for the first time that Soviet penetration in Britain had been far deeper than suspected. The country had experienced spy scandals before, but nothing remotely comparable to this. Here were two prominent officials of the Foreign Office who were believed to have worked for the KGB, who had been discovered by the authorities, and who had fled to

Moscow. I was shattered to learn of the extent of this huge and sinister campaign, designed to undermine Britain's democratic system of government. There could be little doubt as to the political motives by which Burgess and Maclean were guided; by providing intelligence on every possible subject and betraying our agents, their aim had been to install a Communist régime in Britain. Although I was as incredulous as anyone at their treason, I was not afraid on my own account since I had had no contact with either of them on behalf of the KGB. This was an overconfident reaction since I little suspected the carelessness of Burgess but, to start with, there seemed to be no suspicion regarding me on the part of the authorities.

A less dramatic event was my acceptance of an offer of secondment to the Ministry of Supply. Although this Ministry was not highly thought of in Whitehall, I decided to try it out, but the work proved disappointing, consisting of checking the Ministry's record sheet, and offering no scope for formulation of policy. But I had not been there long before I was summoned to meet two visitors from the Security Service. The leader, a trim, dapper figure of around forty who, under a quiet manner proved to be one of the most effective intelligence officers I have ever met, introduced himself as Arthur Martin.

My colleagues at the Ministry explained that a secret letter had been found lying about the office, and that the visitors wished to question me about it, but it soon became clear that this was only the official pretext for the call. The real reason for the meeting was an unsigned letter addressed to me about German re-armament dated about 1939, or just before the war, which ended with the phrase 'Fraternal Greetings', a classic Communist turn of speech. I asked Martin who this was from, and he with a smile said that he expected me to tell him. I had no idea who the writer of the letter could be, but at first suspected that it might have been a student I had known at Glasgow University, though the person in mind had not been, as far as I could remember, a Communist. Martin also pointed out that there was a foreign idiom towards the end of the letter, which made it even more mysterious; and certain linguistic details suggested that the writer was a foreigner. I racked my brains to think who among my acquaintances could have written a letter in that particular vein, but no plausible candidate occurred to me – except perhaps a German I had known at Cambridge, but with whom I never discussed politics; or another German, anti-Nazi but not Communist, whom I had met at the flat of a Foreign Office colleague and with whom I had argued in German for a whole evening about Munich (disingenuously, I recall, taking the Chamberlain line).

The letter had been delivered to my old Warwick Square flat after I had moved out, and had been discovered by a later tenant who returned it to the Post Office. How MI5 came upon it, I do not know, but I remembered that when I was in SIS's Political Section, I had by chance seen my file and read a minute by Anthony Blunt commenting on what must have been this same letter to the effect that one is not necessarily responsible for what other people write to one. Blunt, with piquant irony, had used his position in MI5 to defend me against unjust suspicions.

The letter itself was not too serious, but Martin added that he had found my name in Maclean's personal diary, and proceeded to question me on how well I had known him, and what my impression of him was. The problem here was that the entry marked 'Cairncross' was dated just before he defected to Moscow. I had in fact seen Maclean about that time for after-dinner drinks, so I told Martin everything I knew – which was not much. I started by describing my work with him in the Spanish Department of the Foreign Office in 1937, when I had never noticed anything suspicious about him. We had never discussed politics, but this did not mean, I explained in answer to a shrewd question, that we avoided the subject. It was simply that we preferred to talk about literature, people and, very occasionally, the office. The only political subject I could remember his mentioning was the need for Britain to re-arm. I had kept a loose connection with him thereafter, although without learning about his escapades in Cairo when he had endangered his future career. I had met him again in Paris in 1940 when the Embassy was closing down after the German invasion and the collapse of France. I had also run into him in Whitehall some months before his escape and we had gossiped as old colleagues.

Martin's next inquiry was about my most recent appointment with Maclean. I explained that through my wife I had made the acquaintance of an American couple, Dr and Mrs Chaplin. While Mrs Chaplin was away, I thought that I would arrange a little bachelor party for Maclean, who had recently been appointed head of the American Department of the Foreign Office, to meet Chaplin. This had been shortly before Maclean's sudden departure, and the evening had not been a success.

Chaplin told me the next day that he had been struck by Maclean's depressed, sleepy, almost drugged appearance. I only knew that he had been worried about the imminent birth of a child. I explained that I was unaware of any link he had with the KGB or of his intended defection.

That was the end of my first interview with MI5, and for some time afterwards I heard nothing from Martin. But I must have set something buzzing in his ear for, early the following year when I had returned to the Treasury – to the mutual relief of the Ministry of Supply and myself – I was summoned to meet a new figure from the Security Service, Jim Skardon. He was one of MI5's leading interrogators and the man who had cracked Klaus Fuchs, the atomic spy. A slight swarthy figure, possibly of Greek extraction, Skardon was one of a posse of officials from the Metropolitan Police Special Branch who had been seconded to MI5 at the outbreak of war, and had stayed on.

My interrogation by Skardon was held in an unheated room, since few of the Treasury offices had central heating, and he thoughtfully lit a fire in the open grate. He began the session by saying that the Security Service desperately needed information on the KGB moles and appealed for my help. To tell him about my own activities, or about my controllers, would invite trouble, and I knew nothing about the activities of other agents. The situation, however, provoked a moral dilemma: should I, an average law-abiding man, disclose my underground activity in the interests of the nation and risk a long prison sentence for having, illegally, let our Russian allies have German intelligence on German operations against them? Complete frankness would have meant not only sacrificing myself but abandoning my wife. I thus rejected any thought of confession; but any qualms of conscience I might have felt were, in any case, silenced by what followed.

Having thus broached the issue, Skardon drew from his briefcase a paper which, he said, had come into his possession. He handed it to me and I froze as soon as I recognised my own writing. The document was a photocopy of the hand-written notes I had given to Guy Burgess in July 1939 about British policy towards Poland. In the new context of the Cold War and the defections, I was thunderstruck at this discovery and muttered that I was out of my depth. Skardon simply smiled at my confusion and commented that he was swimming nicely. (MI5, though aided by luck, must be given full marks for their skill in tracking me down as the author of the hand-written notes. Martin's secretary had formerly worked in the Treasury, and recognised my peculiar handwriting.)

At this point I argued that giving information to a colleague, and not very confidential details at that, was not an offence. I denied knowing that Burgess had been a KGB agent, but decided that I had better come clean about my flirtation with Communism, and wrote a statement to that effect. Skardon then read out to me a letter from 'a source in Cambridge' which attested that I had shown every sign of being a faithful Communist until I went down. There was no doubt in my mind as to the source – it was Blunt. Ironically, Skardon had said during the interview that, 'We trust Blunt implicitly.' I was fairly certain that as a consequence of the admission of my flirtation with Communism at Cambridge, I would now be regarded as a dyed-in-the-wool Marxist, to be duly entered on MI5 files as such. Skardon then told me, in his most casual manner and to my great relief, that it had been decided not to prosecute me, but I was called upon to resign from the Treasury, which I gladly did. Realising that Skardon had no hard evidence of my connection with the KGB, I had been evasive to save my skin; but I recognised that this situation might not hold true for much longer.

So far, the only discussion I had held with my controller as to emergency procedures was the possibility of getting to Vienna (to the Consulate in the Russian-occupied Sector), but I had not the slightest desire to arrive at such a ruinous solution or to desert my wife, and at no point expressed any intention of defecting. After my interrogation with Skardon, I put off meeting Modin as I knew that I was bound to be tailed. In the circumstances, however, which left me in a serious financial situation with no savings and without a pension, I was anxious to see whether the KGB could be of any help. I had an emergency procedure for calling a rendezvous with Modin which was to be indicated by a white chalk sign at a particular spot on the kerb, and this I initiated.

On the evening of my KGB appointment, I had dined at the Travellers Club, and as I was going down the steps to the street I noticed, out of the corner of my eye, a porter rushing to the telephone (to call someone at the MI5 Watcher Service, as it turned out). I took a taxi as I felt that the car which the KGB had insisted on my having would be easy to follow. I was, however, tailed to my meeting, which was at the bus station outside an Ealing tube station. I should doubtless not have kept the appointment, but I felt that I had very little to lose, and when I arrived at my destination my suspicions about the tail were confirmed – I at once spotted two suspiciously unoccupied loiterers. I waited a short time, and when no one turned up, I went back home. Modin, too, I learned much later, must have rapidly taken in the position and departed. I never saw the KGB again.

The next day I was summoned by Skardon to another meeting at which I was asked for an explanation. I put forward a threadbare story of an appointment with a girl; and in a climate of scepticism as to my good faith, the matter was dropped, although I have no doubt that I was carefully watched from then onwards. My telephone, too, was tapped, and I was quizzed on various innocent calls. (After this fiasco, MI5 apparently concluded that Modin had been forewarned by some high-powered mole. According to Modin's version, published in 1991 in Moscow, he was sharply reproved by his London superiors for his 'cowardice'. From my own point of view, his prudence was fully justified, for any attempt to contact me that evening would have been disastrous for both of us.)

In the end, luck was on my side, so that I managed to put a good face on my resignation from the Treasury, though my brother Alec remained sceptical of my account. It was also difficult to adopt a disingenuous stance with my wife to whom I had never breathed a word about the KGB. From a Frankfurt Jewish family she was certainly no friend of Hitler, and might even have condoned my actions, but I did not feel inclined to impose such a moral burden on our marriage. I had given it, however, an inauspicious start with my loss of a secure position, and poor and uncertain prospects. I was saved from destitution by generous loans from my brother; but these were short-term and stop-gap measures. However, both my wife and I were keen to settle in Italy, so I sold my car and to that extent, the KGB enabled me to survive. We arranged to let our flat furnished, got together the little money we had and prepared to travel by boat and train to Paris. We stopped off in Switzerland with Gabi's relatives to await the results of my applications for posts at three British Universities, including Oxford, for which Graham Greene offered a reference: 'Dear Claymore. Of course you can use me as a reference if it is worth anything for your application at Oxford.' After reminding me that one should never leave one's job without having another, Lord Hankey also wrote that he would be delighted for me to use his name as a reference for an application to Oxford or UNESCO. I had still hoped to enter academic life but my applications proved unsuccessful, and my hopes of an academic career being dashed, we finally made our way to Rome. I had entered into no agreement with the Security Service, and we had departed openly, legally, and without let or hindrance.

TEN

Confession in Cleveland

With my unsatisfying government career over, I was not only freed from a dull and unpromising job but also finally from the KGB. Gabi and I settled in Italy at a time when it was even more attractive than it is today and I began my twenty-year love affair with that country. Rome in 1952 was a very quiet quasi-provincial city, and even with modest means one could live most agreeably. The openness and spontaneity of the Italian milieu suited both my wife and me, especially as we spoke Italian. We rented rooms in the charming villa of Neapolitan friends in Via dei Pamphili, and my wife, being a highly trained trilingual personal assistant, immediately got a job as secretary at the Food and Agricultural Organisation of the United Nations (FAO).

By great good luck I became the Rome correspondent for the *Economist*, a post that Cecil Sprigge was providentially leaving, and to which I soon added the *Glasgow Herald*. I also became correspondent for the *Observer* International Service and worked for the Canadian Broadcasting Corporation compiling radio reports in English and in French. In addition, there was a rich field of popular, religious and cultural events on which I wrote regular articles. I once went down to Syracuse in Sicily to interview a lady who claimed that she had witnessed a statue of the Virgin shedding tears – this was an Italy that had almost disappeared, and one which I found fascinating. By good fortune, we had escaped the serious financial problems we might have expected and were even able to buy a car. (Incidentally, I was cured of liver trouble caused by bad English fats, by switching to olive oil.)

I supplemented our joint earnings by freelance jobs as a translator and précis writer for the United Nations in Rome and by jaunts to Geneva, where we moved in 1956 to live at Villette par Conches overlooking the lake. A friend at the United Nations in New York then suggested me as Chief Editor at The Economic Council for Asia and the Far East (ECAFE). This was one of six regional UN bodies, Latin America, Africa and Europe all having similar agencies. I was duly appointed and in 1957 we left for Thailand and settled in Bangkok.

I loved the country and the people. Thailand was a land of enchantment, a subtle blend of Indian and Chinese traits. Despite the inevitable growing pains of modernisation the Thais had retained their ready smile, a sense of fun (*sanook*) and their earthy songs: but above all a politeness unknown to the West. A girl who is not known as a raving beauty is not called 'plain' but 'slightly beautiful'. There is no word in the Thai language for 'no' – an answer will always accommodate the desire of the questioner. But perhaps the most notable and enduring characteristic of the Thai people is their tolerance – *Mai pen rai* (it doesn't really matter). Buddhism has always been deeply rooted in the Siamese soul, and thus there are many roads to heaven.

Editing and journalism seemed my natural métier, and in my new post I spent four wonderful years working with delightful people of all nationalities. We had the luxury of a house with a garden, and even an air-conditioned bedroom. I attended conferences in many Asian countries, particularly enjoying visits to Malaysia and Japan: but I still had time, with my gin and lime in the cool of the evening, to research the history of seventeenth-century Siam and the Abbé de Choisy, Louis XIV's eccentric ambassador to that country; and to complete a volume of poems and translations entitled *By a Lonely Sea* (with a foreword by Edmund Blunden), which I published in Hong Kong in 1959. Somerset Maugham, after passing through Bangkok, wrote to me about these translations: 'I read first your poem from the Chinese. I found it charming. I was glad to read Icarus again [my poem 'The Modern Icarus']. You have provided me with a great deal of pleasure.'

On 5 February, 1959 I received a letter from E. V. Rieu, Editor of the Penguin Classics, informing me that Penguin thought very highly of my blank verse translation of Racine's *Phèdre*, which I had published myself in Geneva in 1958, and that they wished to arrange for its publication, along with an introduction by me. I was just leaving for Australia but I wrote to tell him that I would be coming to England in November to take on a literary agent. I proposed in addition two other plays covering different phases of Racine's works. *Phèdre*, *Bérénice* and *Athalie* would give a spread between Greece, Rome and the Bible. I later substituted *Iphigénie* for *Bérénice*, and by 1961, I was able to submit the final draft of what I considered, *sans trop de zèle,* would be something of an event since many considered Racine to be untranslatable.

In 1963 an economist friend suggested I should join him at Karachi on Pakistan's Planning Commission, and I left Bangkok to take up an advisory post as a member of the Harvard Group. My experience of life in the Indian sub-continent was interesting and valuable since I was encouraged to travel extensively. Towards the end of my assignment I heard from Lester Crocker, an American professor who had been a fellow student of mine at the Sorbonne in the early 1930s, and was now an eminent authority on eighteenth-century French literature. He wrote that he was interested in my coming to the United States to replace him as Head of Department for Romance Languages at Western Reserve University in Cleveland, Ohio. The suggestion had come from Professor Raymond Picard, an eminent French scholar and Professor at the Sorbonne with whom I had struck up a close friendship. I welcomed this prospect enthusiastically since I had already written two well-received critical studies of Molière and had always been eager to enter academic life. I was attracted by the opportunity of living in America where I had never set foot, and, in any case, I now needed a job. But I realised that since the British and American security services collaborated closely, the Federal Bureau of Investigation would almost certainly have traces of me in its records. Nevertheless, I decided to take the risk and at once set about obtaining an American visa. Probably because my residence was in Rome before I went to Karachi, my application had to go through the American Consulate in that city. To my surprise, no difficulty was made about granting me the visa: this was just one misleading step in the process whereby I succumbed to the innocent hope that my American venture would turn out all right. It was all the more natural for me to hope, since I have always been lucky in the circumstantial things of life, if not in the essentials – for my wife and I had by now separated. On my return from Pakistan to London I therefore had to fly to Rome to make my visa application. When it finally arrived I left for my new berth with great anticipation and landed in Cleveland in mid-February 1964. Having got so far, I felt that perhaps, as my new post had no political connections, I would be fortunate enough to be able to settle down to a congenial life; and so my basic mood was expectant but essentially fatalistic.

I was given a warm and heartening welcome at the University and I was soon immersed in my lectures on seventeenth-century literature. They were given in French, and it was a pleasure to teach young people eager to learn and develop, but my advice was sometimes found strange. For instance, I suggested to one student who sought guidance on choosing a subject for her thesis that, instead of looking for an issue not yet fully examined, she should find a problem to which available solutions seemed unsatisfactory – a counsel of perfection at variance with the thesis-making machine!

I was delighted to have entered the academic world at a high level, and I was very happy in Cleveland where my colleagues were congenial and the cultural opportunities were outstanding. There was a first-rate orchestra conducted by Sir George Szell, who had been lured over from Glasgow and who put on a wonderful performance of Purcell's *Dido and Aeneas*; a magnificent art museum with an outstanding director, and a local cinema which showed a series of the works of great directors such as Bergman and Kurasawa.

I continued to believe that I could go on without fear that the ghosts of my past would return to haunt me, but I was completely wrong. Around mid-April there was a knock on the door of my room at the Hotel Commodore on Ford Drive and a member of the FBI politely introduced himself. He told me that Arthur Martin of MI5, who had interrogated me back in 1952, would be calling on me shortly. Though he bore bad news, this American official will always leave a pleasant impression in my mind, for somehow he had learned that I had done some poetry translations, and confided to me that his wife was fond of verse, so I presented him with a small volume of mine which I learned had been much appreciated.

Martin arrived a few days after the FBI special agent and, in the twelve years that had passed since I had seen him, he had changed little, and under a quiet exterior he radiated intelligence and efficiency. Of course I was not happy to meet up with MI5 again but, though shocked and nervous, I was glad that at least I had to deal with someone so able. This was the beginning of a long connection with Martin, during which my esteem for him only increased. He lost no time in getting down to business, and at once started to interrogate me. He was calm, efficient and polite, and went straight to the point, confining his questions to those directly related to espionage in exactly the same way as he had done at our last meeting. He advised me, with typical understatement, that I 'had not told him the whole truth' about my involvement in espionage. This remark was enough to convey to me that someone had spoken. My first suspicion was that his source was a defector, but this detail was carefully concealed from me. (His informant was again Anthony Blunt, the man who had organised my recruitment without appearing on the scene himself.)

Whoever had been MI5's informant, it was obvious that the Security Service had something definite to chew on, and by now I was tired of having the carpet sharply removed from under me, being left with no resources, and having to start all over again. What is more, I was determined to make an end of this cat and mouse game once and for all, and even briefly contemplated suicide. Finally, however, I decided to take a strong whisky and make a full confession of my association with the KGB.

Martin did not immediately ask me any penetrating questions, being more interested in practical issues such as the date of my recruitment. This, I explained, had occurred in May 1937, after my entry into the Foreign Office when I had become of interest to the Russians. Martin also asked about the identity of the men concerned in my recruitment, and I named them as James Klugmann, who had effected the introduction and then disappeared, and Otto, the KGB official who had made the initial approach. Martin also dwelt on the periods during which my case officer was absent, the net effect of these absences being, if account was taken of the months when my operations were purely formal, that the KGB derived very little information from me either when I was at the Foreign Office until December 1938, or after I moved to the Treasury.

The other point on which Martin questioned me was my connection with the four members of the Cambridge group. He asked me in particular what my relations were with Maclean, and I repeated what I had told his colleague Skardon. On Burgess he did not query me, no doubt because he was convinced that I was fully aware of his KGB connections which, as I had also told Skardon, was not so. Martin seemed disappointed with the information extracted from me: 'A dull case,' he said. At the same time, he told me that this affair had come before the Cabinet and that, if the news broke, there would be huge headlines. For me, his most important comment was that my confession had been accepted as essentially accurate, which I took to mean that it was in line with other information already in MI5's possession. At the end of his interrogation I offered spontaneously to sign a statement, as I imagined this would be the ritual ending of my confession. To my complete astonishment, Martin said that a great many people had been mixed up in this affair, by which he clearly meant that no such gesture on my part was called for, and that it was planned to keep everything under wraps. Martin then moved on to a more personal note and asked me where my sympathies now lay. I replied that the answer must be fairly obvious, since I had voted with my feet.

Martin was the only MI5 official who tried to understand my mentality (but not my motives, which he took for granted) and who asked perceptive questions going beyond the strictly professional boundaries of his job. He asked me, for example, whether I had ever told anyone else about my KGB connection, and I told him that I had not. But I did not seek to explain that this was partly because the outside world would see only the penal aspect in it, and that I had therefore concealed and denied my involvement. He wondered whether my conscience was more at peace when the Molotov-Ribbentrop Pact had ended. I told him that it was, but did not go into the reasons, which were not quite as he understood them, since I regarded the agreement as almost entirely due to Chamberlain's blindness.

I never discussed with Martin his views on Communism, but it was clear that he saw Russia solely as a threat to capitalism and never as a natural, if difficult, strategic ally on the basis of national self-interest. We did discuss, in passing, the grant of independence to Southern Rhodesia, and Martin had definite views on the ability of the ex-colonies to govern themselves, and was convinced that 'their future was black in every sense of the word'. I wonder what he would say now that the ex-Rhodesians seem to be going ahead as well as could be hoped, whereas the Western phobia about Communism has reduced the neighbouring, and potentially much richer, country of Zaire to a heap of ruins.

Martin's enthusiasm was fired by America rather than by the 'lesser breeds'. He was attached to the United States, but not blindly, because he once referred to America as 'a police state'. He was particularly taken by New York where, he said, the atmosphere was electric. There was no reason, he went on, why I should not stay on in America, since I had committed no offence against that country. I am not sure whether he was sincere, or was just trying to sustain my morale, which had taken a bad knock despite the happy ending to our meeting.

The possibility of my staying on in America was unfortunately to be ruled out but at least I was not extradited to England, for it had been made clear to me by the FBI that I would be arrested at once if I set foot there. 'You know what would happen to you if you went back to London?' an agent asked jokingly. A further FBI concession had been that it did not intend to report my confession to the University and that I would be allowed to serve the last few months of the term and leave America peacefully, provided I went straight to a third country. Most important of all, complete silence would be maintained about my KGB involvement.

The greatest bonus to me at this point was simply the fact that I could go on living at all, for I had fully expected not only to have to make a formal confession, but to be shipped back to England to face trial. Nor had I any illusions about the probable severity of a sentence. England was still suffering from the shock of the third defection of a Cambridge mole to Russia the year before, for Kim Philby had fled in January 1963, and at that point MI5's preconceived ideas about me as just another mole were so strong that I felt unable to argue my case. Had I realised then the implications for the Allies of my transmission of ENIGMA on the Battle of Kursk, my whole attitude, and my willingness to face prosecution, might well have been very different.

A great deal of nonsense has been written about my confession and it is sometimes assumed that I was acting from strength whereas, on the contrary, I felt in an utterly defenceless position. Some molehunters have told me that I should have chanced my luck and denied everything, especially because of the supposed impossibility of extraditing me. This is a quite unrealistic suggestion because the American authorities could always have expelled me on the slightest of pretexts had they so wished. Even in the short run, I would have had to move to another country, find employment and readjust my whole style of living. I cannot stress strongly enough that this was not the first disaster of the kind, but the second, since I had been faced with roughly the same drastic changes with my dismissal from the Treasury. This argument could only be advanced by someone who has not been obliged repeatedly to obtain either an entrance visa or a residence permit. It is not as if the grant of such facilities is on the same basis as the issue of a health certificate. My confession was a gesture of despair whereby I was accepting ruin, since I was prepared to lose everything. Yet, by a supreme irony, I came out of the affair relatively unscathed, at least for a time. After the end of my questioning by the Security Service, the FBI itself naturally wanted to have a statement from me, and this was a bad moment because that very morning I had been to the dentist to have a wisdom tooth extracted, and it was immediately clear to me that I would have to go over the very same ground for the umpteenth time. When I was unwise enough to point this out to the Special Agent interrogating me he replied, justifiably, that I was there to answer his questions, so I did. However, I could not explain the facts of my recruitment to his satisfaction, and the official, on the basis of the information submitted to him, took it for granted that I was a Communist believer. Unfortunately for me, Russia was by that time viewed solely in the light of the Cold War. One FBI man who interviewed me afterwards had completely forgotten that Britain and Russia had been allies for a period of four years during the Second World War. His grasp of history had large gaps in it and he thought that the democracies' main enemy before the war was Russia and not Germany; also, subsequent events had overlaid his recollection of that period, no doubt because at that time he had been a young man in his early twenties. For the rest, he was competent, stuck to the point and, as I learned in subsequent conversation, had the same problems as countless other officials, such as how to afford to put his children through college.

After this final talk, I encountered no further difficulties in arranging for my exit from America, and as it was the end of the semester I was lucky enough to find a place on a special flight for academics direct from New York to Paris. The FBI was taking no chances, and a hardfaced G-man summoned me to present myself at the airport just before I embarked. Thus it was with immense relief that I landed in Paris, and no longer felt in imminent danger of ruin and disaster. Despite the unambiguous behaviour of the FBI, I wanted to clarify my status with the American authorities, and I therefore made an application to the American Consulate in Paris to be allowed to return to the United States. Martin's assurances, however, proved worthless, for I was refused. In its reply, the Consulate listed six offences which I had committed against the United States, but I cannot say that I found the charges particularly alarming. Having afterwards destroyed the letter, as I never liked to have such compromising things hanging around, the only serious accusation that I can recall was that I had been a member of a secret Russian organisation, the KGB.

After a short plunge into the atmosphere of my student days, I left Paris for Aix-en-Provence to spend two weeks with my friend Raymond Picard. From there I wrote to the University and, on the pretext of ill-health, regretfully resigned. I had been extremely happy in Cleveland and had never enjoyed a post so much.

I then took the train to Rome.

ELEVEN

Enter Mr P and Mrs R

I had many friends in Rome and soon found an apartment in Monteverdi Vecchio, the old part of Rome overlooking Trastevere, and eventually got a new job as editor with the UN's FAO.

Soon after my return, however, I was contacted again by MI5, and Arthur Martin and his colleague Peter Wright flew out to interrogate me on some of the factual details about my confession. Nothing of special note arose in these discussions, but two curious incidents occurred. I was sitting with Martin at an outdoor café, when we were approached unblushingly by an unknown intruder who took a photograph of the two of us. We were both equally surprised, and concluded that the stranger must be an American. Martin told me that he would check on the episode and, if our guess was correct, he would tell the Americans to lay off which, as far as I know, they did. Martin was not involved in the second incident, and I did not report it to him. At Rome's airport, when I was about to fly to Paris, I was asked by an airport reception clerk to show him my passport, which they had never asked to see before. I reluctantly handed it to him with a look, and he gave it back after flicking through it. I had no doubt that he was an American agent looking for visas to suspicious destinations such as Helsinki and Prague, which were common stops on the way to Moscow.

Soon after these episodes, Martin branched off from our usual discussions to ask me whether I was not angry with Klugmann for the sneaky part he had played in effecting my recruitment to the KGB back in 1937. Would I be willing to testify against him if the possibility arose of bringing him to trial? I replied that I would have no hesitation in bearing witness against him. This question was taken a step further by Peter Wright, and the possibility of complete immunity was held out, plus the continuation of confidentiality and the freedom to visit England if I succeeded in pinning down Klugmann as one of the architects of my involvement with the KGB. I did not know it at the time, but any such cooperation was bound to carry immunity irrespective of the outcome of my gesture. (This concession appears to have been unauthorised and gave rise to a discussion between Wright and Sir Roger Hollis, Director-General of MI5, as part of an internal MI5 feud.)

As it turned out, I did not have to testify against Klugmann publicly, which would have represented a very high price to have to pay, given the resultant publicity about my own KGB activities. It happened like this: we met in 1967 at a hotel in London, where I was being put up by MI5. I was informed by Wright beforehand that Klugmann was a very disappointed man since he had not risen as high in the Party apparatus as he had hoped. For my part, I was aware that Klugmann had not always followed the rigid Party line, for he had supported the heretical Chinese right up to the moment of their break with the Soviets. I did not enjoy meeting Klugmann again. He had changed little during the thirty years since I had last seen him, except for having put on a little weight. I had to make an effort to pretend a certain restraint, for the recollection of his shock tactics in Regent's Park was still green in my memory after all that time. My mood was not improved when he immediately said that he had been concerned about me. He certainly had good reason to be worried after all I had been through. However, I had to suppress my feelings until after he had eaten well, as he was definitely fond of a good meal, and I had been carefully advised by MI5 to wait until he had been wined and dined before trying to extract a confession from him.

After lunch, in which I skated around non-committal issues, I waited until we were out of the restaurant and then taxed him with the unsavoury role which he had played in involving me with the KGB. Chapman Pincher, in his rather inaccurate account of my meeting with Klugmann (*Their Trade is Treachery*) relates that my former acquaintance laughed in my face. On the contrary, he reacted very nervously and declared, in an obvious falsehood, that he did not know anything about the Russian agent present at the Regent's Park meeting. When, in a final appeal, I reminded him of our common opposition to Nazism, he simply dwelt on the importance of the communist movement among the students at Cambridge at that time, and all I could extract from him was the admission that he had been asked by various friends or acquaintances to come forward and report his activities to MI5. However, he felt no obligation to do so and it was clear that my approach had been a failure.

After the Klugmann episode, I had various talks with Wright and others in Rome in order to clarify some points of detail in my confession but otherwise silence reigned for almost seven years.

During this time I continued to earn my keep at FAO. My work consisted of extensive and often unofficial editorial tasks, usually done for colleagues. I was also responsible for preparing papers for the International Fund for Agricultural Development and, as senior economics adviser, writing the FAO's biannual reports evaluating the organisation's performance. Many developing countries believed that 'western prosperity' for them lay in the development of industry. I addressed this issue in two studies, comparing traditional methods of agriculture (as for instance in China) with modern industrial production and the different effects they have on population structure. My most valuable work, however, lay in the composition of two pamphlets. The first, *Things to Come* (1974), was for the Sixth United Nations World's Food Conference, and dealt with the world food crisis and women's role in solving these problems. As I have always been interested in women's rights and demography I was also asked to help in producing the second pamphlet, *The Missing Half* (1975), a monograph for The Women's Year Conference in Mexico. Although in re-drafting the text I had retained only ten lines of the original version by the two women entrusted with the assignment, for expediency it was attributed to them but 'with the collaboration of John Cairncross'.

Nothing new of importance in my relations with MI5 happened until I received a letter in 1973 from a Mr P in MI5 indicating that some points in my case were beginning to bother them and inviting me to submit to a further interrogation, this time in London. All my contacts with MI5 were with him from then on, and we met in a room on the ground floor of the old War Office building in Whitehall, opposite Horseguards Parade, where MI5 traditionally conducted interviews with outsiders. The extraordinary scene which follows is not,

MINISTRY OF DEFENCE
Room 055 Old War Office Building Whitehall London SW1A 2EU
Telephone 01-930 9400 ext. 0393

J Cairncross Esq
Via Armando Spadini 16
Parioli
Rome

Your reference

Our reference

Date   31 July 1973

Dear M. Cairncross

    Thank you very much indeed for taking the trouble you obviously have to prepare and to send us through the channel I suggested a record of the thoughts you have had since we last met.

    I am sure you will not take it amiss when I say that in many cases the inferences you have drawn from points arising in our discussions are well wide of the mark. It is nevertheless useful to us to know your thinking and I hope that when we next meet having this knowledge will help clarify those aspects of the past which remain unresolved. This is I know something we both want.

    I look forward to seeing you again when you are next here.

Yours sincerely

unfortunately, taken from a third-rate comedy about espionage, but records extracts from an actual interrogation.

Naturally the office was wired for sound and conversations were recorded, yet Mr P, in a brave attempt to save appearances, pretended to take notes, with quite unconvincing zeal. At this meeting he was accompanied by a very personable young lady named Stella Rimington who was dressed elegantly in trousers (and who later became Director-General of MI5). The two officials divided the roles of the good and the bad cop in dealing with me, and Mr P at once let loose a storm of criticism. My case, he explained, was like an onion, in which one layer after another revealed all sorts of hidden iniquities. Mr P showed me a letter from 'Wilhelm' to an address in Greece, from which it appeared that he was in touch with a Communist intelligence agency, and in which he referred to certain papers, presumably British designs. Mr P never said so explicitly, but implied that I had supposedly given these designs to 'Wilhelm'. I remembered the ex-*Luftwaffe* pilot whom I had met briefly in Paris because I had been quizzed about him on joining SIS: he had claimed to have invented a new radar device and I had referred him to the proper Ministry. Mr P sneered at my patriotism in putting the German in touch with the British authorities, and elaborated on the danger of my move: what a prize, he speculated, if 'Wilhelm' had managed to establish contact with Robert Watson-Watt, the radar expert at the Air Ministry! It was in vain that I protested that I had only put him in touch with the Ministry and that it was up to that body to decide how to handle the case. If I were a KGB agent, as Mr P supposed, I would have channelled all this through my Soviet case officer and not through some unknown German, and a small fish at that. Among the other innumerable inaccurate charges in which Mr P indulged was that in which my old Paris friend Etienne Tamboury was but one of my apparently inexhaustible supply of customers for secret information. Mr P next asked me why I had not kept my 1937 appointment with Burgess in Paris, and expressed surprise at my explanation that, instinctively, I had made no special effort to see him.

The next and even more stupefying charge was that I had been shielding someone at my first interrogation in 1952. I replied that I had had quite enough trouble shielding myself without bothering about other people. (It turned out that I was supposed to be shielding Blunt, an uproarious idea!) But this was not all. It seemed that my willingness to confess fully in 1964 had aroused the deepest suspicions of Peter Wright's successors at MI5, who worked on the familiar basis that if a trick is played on them once, it is bound to be repeated. Just as Philby is supposed to have spun his British interrogator a tall story to cover his defection from Beirut in 1963, I must have invented an ingenious story about my KGB experiences, having of course first been warned by some mysterious KGB Superspy in MI5. When I told them that I had felt cornered when I made my disclosures in Cleveland, as indeed I was, I was met with the utmost scepticism. MI5's scenario for this case was the purest fantasy, but it was based on internal office politics, the official MI5 line now being that Wright and Martin were sheer troublemakers, and not very efficient ones at that, who had let such dangerous characters as Cairncross slip through the net.

After the bad cop routine came the good one, and Mrs Rimington questioned me closely about my visit to Cambridge in 1936 to meet Louis MacNeice in Blunt's rooms with Burgess. This was taken as a meeting of the KGB hard-liners to plan the next moves in their strategy, whereas in fact it had been the preparation of my own unwitting recruitment. I was asked, for example, at what hotel I had spent Saturday night, and it took me quite an effort to remember that we worked on Saturday mornings in those days, and so my outing had been confined to a Sunday. Then I had to give an account of my journey back to London by train with Burgess, and I was told by Mrs Rimington that, according to him, he had recruited me on precisely this occasion. I was asked what we talked about, and I told her. All of this was intended by MI5 to show that I was far more deeply interwoven into the KGB's network than hitherto I had been prepared to admit. I eventually learned the origin of these fables: former spy Goronwy Rees.

Lastly, I was accused by my two inquisitors of having yielded to Soviet inducements and hence been willing to work for them for mercenary considerations. Considering that the only inducement suggested to me had consisted of the Chicherin ploy at my recruitment, whereby I would rise to become head of the Foreign Office, this was simply laughable. For some reason, no doubt to blacken me, I was portrayed as being very close to the Russians. The suggestion in any case did not make any sense, for the Russians did nothing for me when my usefulness was at an end. Whatever the value of my services to them, they knew that I was not a true believer and treated me accordingly. The fact is that for Mr P I was simply a Communist fanatic, like the four famous Cambridge moles with whom I have been wrongly associated at every stage in my career, and no amount of disproofs and denials have so far been able to remove the stigma. I did try to correct some of the main errors, and whilst my arguments may have been cogent, my tone was certainly one of unmistakable fury. By now I had completely lost my patience. 'I get the picture,' I said sarcastically, 'of myself standing in Piccadilly distributing top secret papers to all and sundry, with hardly time to go to the lavatory.' The charges, I concluded, were grotesque. This brought the meeting to an end, and I heard no more from Mr P or the elegant Mrs R.

*

There were now clearly different factions in MI5 for, sometime after Mr P's philippic, I was summoned to another meeting at the War Office in a larger room. Mr P and Mrs R were absent, but all the other top brass of the agency appeared to be present. The chairman was reserved and apologetic, and explained the whole bother, rather lamely, as being due to 'the background'. I forbore from trying to explain a complex case in a few minutes, but I was sorely tempted when a Scot (and I do not know what he was doing in such solidly English company) asked me whether I did not feel discriminated against in this whole case. I replied that this factor had indeed obscured the agency's understanding of several points, but I was so relieved at not having to face the usual firing squad that I did not let fly. This kind of retort can only be delivered as a whole and on paper: the verbal refutation can come only when the case for the accused has been presented and can be analysed calmly and at leisure.

Following these interrogations by Mr P and Mrs R I realised that the top people in the Security Service had not liked my friendship with Arthur Martin and Peter Wright – the former had been transferred to MI6 and the latter retired in 1976 – and that a new broom was now sweeping through MI5.

TWELVE

MI5 Throws Me to the Winds

In August of 1976 I retired from FAO. I was now 63 and living in Parioli, a quiet residential part of Rome where I planned to dedicate myself to the serious business of spending a happy old age, which would console me for at least some of the trials that had attended my ill-starred attempt to temper the world disaster let loose by Hitler's fury and Chamberlain's folly. I thus devoted myself to various research projects, including essays for academic journals and a novel, and I therefore travelled less. Neither Wright nor Martin had made a firm promise that I would be allowed to enter Britain again, but despite my lack of success with Klugmann in 1967, MI5 had kept its word regarding confidentiality and I had visited England on at least three occasions. These included (in addition to attending my brother's sixtieth birthday party in 1971) my home leave on retirement in 1976, and a Trinity College old boys' commemoration dinner at Cambridge in 1977 at which I met again Sir John Colville, who had been a year my senior at Trinity and who had joined the Foreign Office a year after me. Ironically, once an ardent pro-Chamberlainite, he had later become Winston Churchill's wartime Assistant Private Secretary and later still Private Secretary to Princess Elizabeth.

In 1979 another bombshell exploded on the British public with the appearance of Andrew Boyle's book *The Climate of Treason* which led to the subsequent public unmasking by Prime Minister Margaret Thatcher of the 'fourth man' of the Cambridge moles, Sir Anthony Blunt. The pressure was on the Government to reveal details about Blunt, Surveyor of the Queen's Pictures, and the press immediately assailed Buckingham Palace. There, the eager journalists were distracted by Sir John Colville, who sought to rescue the Palace's reputation by boasting of his role in putting MI5 on to another KGB spy who had worked in the Foreign Office. Without actually giving a name, he provided them with sufficient leads, and it took reporters only three days to identify me. Colville's revelations were based on an entry in an old diary – the lunch appointment with me in 1939 when we had discussed British policy towards Germany, my notes on which were found in Burgess's trunk in 1951. On 18 November, 1979 *The Sunday Times* accordingly blazoned the news under the headline 'Churchill's man reveals yet another Soviet Spy'.

A month later, in my Rome apartment on a Saturday, a melodious female voice on the telephone asked me if I was John Cairncross. When I said I was, the voice rang off. It was an old ruse and it worked. An hour later, my door bell rang, and two reporters from *The Sunday Times*, David Leitch and Barrie Penrose, pushed their way past me, explaining that they had been speaking with John Colville. I then reluctantly gave an interview in order to clarify my position. I denied knowing Burgess from my Cambridge days, denied knowing that he was a Soviet agent, and denied supplying him with diplomatic and foreign policy material. I then disappeared for Christmas to Switzerland and missed the article's appearance on the following day, 23 December.

Soon after, in early January, I received a message from the *Sunday Times* journalist Marjorie Wallace asking me to ring her at her home because she had an important message for me. When I rang her she asked me whether I would give her an interview to present the 'other side'. I understood this to mean that I could explain the kind of person I was, my interests, the way I lived, my literary activities and so forth, and so I foolishly agreed to meet her.

I got hold of and finally read the *Sunday Times* of 23 December early in February. It appeared with the double headlines 'I was spy for Soviets' and 'The high-flier who spied for Guy Burgess'. The article itself went further and said I had 'continued to do so at least until the outbreak of the Second World War'. Since the paper represented me in a hideous light, I called up and cancelled my forthcoming appointment with Ms Wallace, who, however, insisted that she was coming anyway. Our mid-February meeting resembled an MI5 grilling but lacked that agency's skill, tact and polish. (When Andrew's book burst on the scene in 1990, Ms Wallace cashed in on her interview manqué with a piece misleadingly headed 'The spy who almost loved me'.) On the same day

I wrote to the editor of the *Sunday Times* (delivering my letter to their Rome office) pointing out the numerous inaccuracies in the paper's December article and denying the charges. I also drafted a letter which they might publish, and on 23 February I submitted a shorter and less argumentative one. Not until two months later, on 24 April, did I receive a letter from the *Sunday Times* refusing to publish my denial and disingenuously defending the paper's action. I was forced to take the matter to the Press Council, but only in October 1980 did the paper print my letter – with the following half-hearted apology: 'the *Sunday Times* regrets any distress caused by certain aspects of the presentation of this story.' (My 'distress' had been considerably alleviated by a letter from Graham Greene: 'I am so glad that you have survived events! I was a bit puzzled because none of the photographs looked in the least like you and only the address tallied. What puzzled me too was that the papers hadn't got on at all to your connection with Section V.')

Colville's 'revelation' and the resulting press campaign were bad enough, but at least the leak had been limited to my notes to Burgess, even if their context had been misunderstood. But worse was to come: Chapman Pincher published *Their Trade is Treachery* in 1981 based on intelligence provided by the then retired Peter Wright. This collaboration revealed copious details of Soviet penetration of British Intelligence and provided a totally inaccurate account of my life and activities. *Their Trade is Treachery* was not banned despite its numerous revelations of secret MI5 matters and the Government's knowledge of Pincher's link with Wright, which, in my opinion, gravely breached the Official Secrets Act. Confronted with a host of serious errors, I was placed in a most unenviable situation: if I tried to refute or correct statements, I would be contravening my 1964 agreement with MI5.

Convinced that Colville's intervention had not been unprompted, I reflected on the promise of confidentiality given to me by the Security Service after my 1964 confession. Our arrangement must have been at least partially based on MI5's desire to keep Blunt's involvement with the KGB out of public knowledge for as long as possible, he being the main and indeed the only witness who could give evidence against me. Certainly if I had been put on trial, it would have been impossible to keep the details of Blunt's offences from the public, whatever the precautions taken in the court itself.

But now that Blunt's espionage activities were known, and since the

Government had taken no action against Pincher, I decided that this tolerance was an indication that MI5 was no longer interested in my complete silence. I therefore decided to sue Pincher for libel, and contacted a lawyer in London with a view to taking legal action. It was clear that any hope of cooperation from MI5 was slender; and when I discussed the matter on the telephone privately with Arthur Martin my doubts were reinforced tenfold. In preparing to sue Pincher, I had wanted to come to England but I was now told by MI5 that I would not be allowed entry. A lawsuit would certainly have been a headliner and explosive, and I eventually dropped any intention of raising the charges in public as I could well understand that an attempt to take Pincher to court would cause embarrassment to the Government. I was, however, surprised that conditional immunity, including confidentiality, had now in fact been withdrawn without any indication to me, for I might easily have tried to visit my friends in England and been arrested.

I learned more about the important issue of immunity from Pincher's *Their Trade is Treachery* and *Too Secret Too Long* (1984). He states, in the latter, that I had been told I would be allowed to return to Britain 'for a limited period without fear of arrest' if I were to confront Klugmann:

> a dispensation to which Hollis [Director-General of MI5] apparently agreed without securing the permission of either the Attorney General or the Director of Public Prosecutions. It would have been routine practice for Hollis to have taken the advice of MI5's legal advisors and, if they interpreted the law as Sir Michael Havers was to do in 1981, Hollis would have been told that the offer to Cairncross could be construed as an inducement which would prohibit future prosecution if he accepted it. Whether or not this was made clear to Cairncross remains secret.

I can confirm that it was never stated that if I pinned down Klugmann I would be granted immunity from prosecution and not just a maintenance of silence: Peter Wright had suggested that we would have to proceed step by step. There was no need to wonder why Blunt, with his 'old boy connections', had been offered immunity in view of the precious information he could give MI5 about KGB penetration. Philby too had been offered immunity, but chose to defect, whereas I was expected to 'work my passage home'. I had no desire to settle in Britain, but I was of course anxious to be able to travel freely. This vital question of immunity had been interpreted by the Attorney General himself in a debate in the House of Commons on 12 November, 1981:

> Generally apart from the question of whether it would be right for the Crown to take the initiative in naming a man as a spy when there was no evidence on which to prosecute him, it seems to be that anonymity should usually be inherent in the granting of immunity.

It had not occurred to me in 1964 to press for immunity, and now even the promise of confidentiality seemed to be evaporating. Luckily, there existed the right of freedom from extradition on Official Secrets grounds – a fact which, ironically, I had learned from Pincher's book.

Pincher's blunders started many historians of wartime Intelligence off on the wrong track. His errors about myself are too many to enumerate in detail. He starts off by informing the reader that my notes found in Burgess's trunk confirmed an 'affair inside the Treasury', and goes on to portray me as a typical 'scholarship boy', stating that I had 'contritely' pleaded poverty as an explanation to MI5 for my actions. I was supposedly convinced that 'Soviet style Communism was the only way of securing social justice'. And I had told MI5 'with some pride' that I had supplied the vital information which enabled the Russians to win the Battle of Kursk (when I had actually learned about my role in that battle from his book). He argued that my behaviour in this context was 'reprehensible in the extreme', for had the Russians leaked knowledge of the real origins of my information to the Germans, I 'would have been the most damaging spy of the war'. He supported this accusation by putting forward the ludicrous assertion that German officers in touch with the KGB who wished to take out personal insurance against the possibility of German defeat, might have been given information about ULTRA 'deliberately to hold up the British and American advance while they [the Russians] overran most of Europe'.

Pincher's assertion that I 'blew' four moles was particularly repulsive. I never had any knowledge of other agents and had not the slightest evidence against anyone. Pincher was equally confused when he wrote that I had admitted, while at SIS, to providing the KGB with a continuous reading of the allied plans concerning the future of Yugoslavia. I never actually worked on Yugoslavian affairs, nor did I have any contact with Klugmann, who did work on Yugoslav affairs from his office in the southern Italian city of Bari. My work at SIS was strictly that of editor and at no point did I have contact with or knowledge of SIS or SOE agents, both being handled by an entirely different unit. (I was later urged by some Americans to 'come clean' over the information I supposedly had on Klugmann and had to threaten them with a lawsuit to get them to lay off.)

Also I had received an interesting letter in 1984 from a lady who, at Bletchley, had processed Yugoslav material during the war and was researching SOE in Cairo and Yugoslavia. She especially wanted to learn why so much intelligence material to and from Draza Mihajloviç (the anti-Communist General fighting the Germans in the mountains of Yugoslavia) seemed to have gone astray; and why Klugmann had kept such remarkably inaccurate maps of partisan operational areas which he had apparently shown to officials in support of switching allegiance from the Chetniks to Josip Broz's (Tito's) Communist Partisans. I replied that, thanks to Pincher, some people had me hopelessly mixed up with Klugmann.

But Pincher's main source, Peter Wright, was to produce his own book in 1987: *Spycatcher*. At least neither of these two authors tried to play up my role as the key figure or as a Fifth Man in a Cambridge ring. But I have no reason to defend Wright, whose notorious book not only revealed to the whole world delicate state secrets but gave a completely false account of my case. My relations with Wright and Martin were always cordial and I never felt that Wright had any animus against me. (In fact, during one of our talks, Wright sounded me out about helping his son to get a job at FAO in Rome.) I was therefore surprised that he chose to portray me as an ideological fanatic and described me as openly acknowledging my Communism in 1979, whereas whenever our conversations had turned to the Soviet problem I had left him under no doubt as to the nature of my views – which were certainly not pro-Communist.

Pincher's and Wright's books certainly did harm to Britain's national interests. Apart from their breach of secrecy and their inaccuracies, there was a very unpleasant aspect about their disclosures. This was the origin of these disclosures, for they did not spring from nowhere. With the unmasking of Anthony Blunt as the 'Fourth Man', the molehunters had started their search for a Fifth Man. This was based on some hint leaked to them of KGB defector Anatoli Golitsyn's erratic account of a Ring of Five (a concept he first brought to the West in 1961). The most prominent subject of popular suspicion had been ex-MI5 executive Lord Rothschild, who had done brilliant and courageous anti-sabotage work for MI5 during the war but had also been a great friend of Kim Philby. Wright rejected the proposal that his friend Victor Rothschild could have engaged in espionage on the grounds of his patriotic work for MI5. Rothschild had however apparently panicked and, to deflect attention from himself and ward off the personal attacks he anticipated, had (in breach of the Official Secrets Act for which the authorities would have been fully justified in prosecuting) arranged for Chapman Pincher, working on material provided by Wright (although few knew his source at the time), to publish *Their Trade is Treachery*. In his book, Pincher put forward Wright's theory that the Director-General of MI5, Sir Roger Hollis, had been a KGB agent. Hollis was thus rolled into the ragbag of those suspected of being undetected Russian agents which at the time included the journalist Sefton Delmer, Sir Rudolf Peierls, the Berlin-born professor of physics, and the Cambridge don Andrew Gow.

Unfortunately for Rothschild, Wright made the admission in *Spycatcher* that Golitsyn had identified Lord and Lady Rothschild as a pair of KGB agents, codenamed DAVID and ROSA. (This had been discovered in early SIGINT traffic deciphered long after the war.) The possibility is that Golitsyn erroneously fastened on to them simply because the names were Jewish, but despite an anguished appeal to Mrs Thatcher in *The Times*, Rothschild was never cleared of suspicion and never earned 'his passage home' with the Government.

These events were the prologue to an attempt to dispose of discussion of the mystery concerning a KGB mole inside the Security Services. Rothschild, through Pincher, had provided the first documented instance known to me of the confusion between the Superspy and the Fifth Man – a confusion that now reigned in the British public's mind as the two were rolled together into a kind of bogeyman of the espionage world, the mysterious Mr X.

The Blunt scandal would inevitably affect many of those whom he had manipulated, and it was obvious that I had been deliberately implicated. It therefore seemed to me that by leaking my KGB connection, and describing my notes to Burgess as a KGB operation, MI5 had in effect thrown me to the winds. But nobody had as yet been thrown to the wolves.

THIRTEEN

The Superspy

The existence of a Russian mole in MI5 has remained the great skeleton in Britain's wartime and post-war intelligence cupboard. He is alleged to have worked for the Russians from at least 1942 up until around 1963, and his destructive effectiveness increased, the evidence suggests, as he climbed the career ladder. But the debate in MI5 on his existence was kept secret from the public until 1981, when it was asserted by Chapman Pincher in *Their Trade Is Treachery* that the prime suspect had been none other than MI5's Director-General, Sir Roger Hollis, who had joined the organisation in 1938 and had retired in 1965.

Their Trade Is Treachery was only the first of a spate of publications dealing with the vexed problem of hostile penetration of the Security Service. In 1984 came a much more detailed investigation, again by Pincher, entitled *Too Secret, Too Long;* and in 1987 Wright returned to the charge in *Spycatcher,* with a full description from his inside vantage-point of the internal battle that had raged within MI5 on this question, especially for the period up to 1981.

The Establishment had always contested the anti-Hollis charges and had even tried to ban *Spycatcher* but could not openly respond to the disturbing allegation that British security had been penetrated for so long, and at the top, by Russian Intelligence. A defence of Hollis would bring out into the open many delicate matters which were not for the public ear, and the controversy might have gone no further had it not been for the collaboration between Christopher Andrew and Oleg Gordievsky. Their book *KGB: The Inside Story*, had the effect of serving as a mouthpiece for MI5 and the Establishment by almost surreptitiously presenting a case for exonerating Hollis from the charge of being the Superspy, while carefully avoiding discussion of the case as put forward by Wright and Pincher. In addition, MI5 would improve its somewhat tarnished image as a result of the enumeration of its successes, of which Gordievsky's career was presented as a striking example.

The naming of me by Andrew as the Fifth Man in a Ring of Five was, therefore, an attempt to reassure the public and deflect attention from the allegations against Hollis. Andrew's argument (which appears in the unsigned introduction to his book) was simple: Hollis, the former head of the Security Service had been accused of being the Fifth Man of the Cambridge Ring, but Gordievsky claimed to have seen in the KGB's secret archives that this sinister figure was none other than a certain Cairncross. Andrew's defence of Hollis was picked up by three eminent members of the Establishment, Lords Armstrong, Dacre and Annan. Armstrong in his letter to *The Times*, published on 2 November, 1990, set out the argument in its most explicit form. Hollis, he wrote, had been accused by Pincher in 1981 of being the Fifth Man: but as Gordievsky had now shown that Hollis was not the Fifth Man, it followed that Hollis could not have been a Russian agent.

Lord Armstrong's remarkable gifts as an administrator were already in evidence when he was my assistant in the Treasury just after the war, but he has been unfortunate in his encounters with the world of Intelligence. His contribution to the brief prepared for Mrs Thatcher by MI5 for her defence in Parliament in 1981 against Pincher's accusations bears little trace of his talents, and he was badly mauled by Malcolm Turnbull, the young Australian lawyer who defended Wright during the *Spycatcher* court case in Sydney. Admittedly Armstrong was badly let down by his superiors on that occasion, but no outside pressure seems to have been applied when he came to draft his letter to *The Times*, which was headed 'The identity of the Fifth Man'. After accepting without more ado Gordievsky's identification of me, he wrote in all seriousness: 'Since "the five" were always a KGB category, Mr Gordievsky's testimony on this point carries great weight.' He then came to the nub of his argument which was: 'What Mr Gordievsky's testimony has done is virtually to destroy the case for thinking that Sir Roger Hollis might have been a Soviet agent.'

I met the respected Oxford historian, Lord Dacre, when he was plain Hugh Trevor-Roper and did distinguished work on SIGINT for SIS. I came across him again in Oxford and later in Rome and I even consulted him about a book on Thailand that I was writing. In the course of our exchange of letters, he took a very complimentary view of my knowledge and writings. In his review of *KGB: The Inside Story* which appeared in the *Sunday Telegraph* of 21 October, 1990 and was entitled 'The real Damage done by the Fifth Man', he made a clear distinction between me and the other moles but in somewhat uncomplimentary terms – I lacked their glamour. He admitted that the Russians obtained valuable ULTRA information from me which many at the time (including Churchill) would have wished them to have. His main point, however, was that until the Cold War little harm had been done directly by the 'five' through the sabotage of British Intelligence, whereas they had left behind them 'a poison of suspicion' which had infected the 'somewhat stifling atmosphere of Intelligence' and of which 'the infamous campaign mounted by Peter Wright against Sir Roger Hollis was the climax'.

He drew up a list of trusted and respected men, including Hollis, who had been denounced as the Fifth Man, but he attributed this campaign to the 'intrepid huntsmen of the missing mole'. Here we again plunge into an undergrowth of error and confusion. He mixed up throughout, quite unjustifiably, the two separate ideas of Fifth Man and Superspy and in fact went much further than the other Establishment commentators by merging the two concepts: I became, by a remarkable feat of acrobatics, both the Fifth Man and the Superspy. It seemed to be an article of faith with him that, since I had been denounced as the Fifth Man, Hollis was to be let off that particular hook. Thus, the charge that he was a Soviet mole must be rejected even though he was suspected of being the Superspy, not just by outsiders, but by his own colleagues.

Lord Annan, the noted historian, in his article for *The Times Saturday Review* of 20 October, 1990, described *KGB: The Inside Story* as 'the most fascinating of all spy books' and accepted uncritically all Andrew's assertions. Like Armstrong and Dacre, his main contention was that, given Gordievsky's denunciation of me as the Fifth Man, Hollis, who had been accused of filling that role, was therefore automatically exonerated from the charge of espionage. Thus, the separate questions of KGB penetration of the Security Service and the figure known as the Fifth Man had now become hopelessly intertwined and confused.

*

It is certainly true that, for some time after the unmasking of Blunt in 1979, general confusion reigned about the Fifth Man and the Superspy, the last sought-after Soviet mole in British Intelligence, but by 1983 this amalgamation had been dispelled except in the minds of the uninformed public. In the *Listener* of 23 July, 1982, Andrew had, in fact, demonstrated either by brilliant deduction or on the strength of inside information based on the Blunt confession, that there had never been a Ring of Five but only of four; and therefore concluded that Hollis could not be the Fifth Man. In presenting his case in 1990, Andrew also referred to 'Chapman Pincher's sensational allegation that the Fifth Man was Sir Roger Hollis'. But, neither Pincher nor Wright had ever mentioned Hollis as a member of the Cambridge ring, not least because he had been at Oxford. (They had always pointed to Alister Watson, a Cambridge-educated scientist.) The Fifth Man was regarded as having been educated at Cambridge and run by the KGB, whereas the Superspy was, initially at least, a GRU agent operating from Oxford, to which much of MI5 had been evacuated in 1940 – their offices to Blenheim Palace and their personnel to Keble College. What Wright and Pincher had constantly asserted, to the acute embarrassment of the MI5 hierarchy, was that Hollis could indeed have been the major Russian agent in MI5.

What has now been demolished, on the basis of Yuri Modin's unambiguous evidence, is the whole concept of the Fifth Man. Thus when, at the end of his review, Dacre claimed that 'the exposure of the Fifth Man should enable us to breathe a purer air', his confidence was sadly misplaced, for it was almost inevitable that, once the convenient simulacrum of the Fifth Man had been eliminated, the Superspy, hitherto wrapped up in mothballs, was likely to take on a new lease of life. The two figures are like the little figures on a Swiss clock, one of which comes out to strike the hour as the other goes in.

Guy Liddell, formerly MI5's Deputy Director-General, was also included on Dacre's list. His inclusion was particularly unjustified because in *Spycatcher* Wright had denounced the suspicions concerning him as palpably absurd; and there is no evidence that Wright ever changed his opinion. In any case, Liddell left MI5 as early as 1952 solely because of his disappointment at insufficient promotion, whereas the Superspy was believed to be active inside the Security Service for a further decade. I can only trace attacks on Liddell as having been a potential Superspy to John Costello's *Mask of Treachery*, which was published in 1988.

In my view, Liddell and the others were only 'springes to catch woodcocks', and the real subject of the debate remains Roger Hollis. It cannot be repeated too often that Wright's persistence, in the face of constant obstruction by his superiors, in pressing for a thorough examination of KGB penetration of MI5 by a Superspy codenamed ELLI, as he was known in 1945 to defector Igor Gouzenko, was based on a considerable weight of evidence. This cannot be countered by adducing Wright's undoubted excesses in other cases and his unfortunate meddling in British politics. And the issue has little, if anything, to do with the question of the Fifth Man, either substantively or chronologically.

Annan must have been reading the same books as Dacre for he too, includes Guy Liddell in his list of people wrongly accused of being the Fifth Man, but he adds a third figure, that of Graham Mitchell. Here Annan was following the Establishment party line, for Hollis and Mitchell were the primary suspects of being the top-level Russian moles inside MI5. Mitchell was eventually cleared by his colleagues, but Hollis was interrogated even after his retirement. Annan's argument was perhaps even more unbalanced in his examination of Peter Wright's *Spycatcher* in the *New York Review of Books* of 27 September, 1987 in which he asserted that Hollis let Klaus Fuchs continue his work on the atomic bomb project, despite his well-known Communist associations, only because of pressure from the key scientist, Sir Edward Appleton, who contended that Fuchs's collaboration was vital. But in his biography *The Truth about Hollis*, his biographer William J. West notes that Hollis cleared Fuchs as many as six times, and concludes: 'Particularly damaging was Hollis's clearance of all the Soviet agents so far known who were infiltrated into the atom bomb project.'

Annan gave another reason for Hollis's innocence by his acceptance of Gordievsky's curious identification of Leo Long as ELLI, a thesis which most molehunters reject entirely. Just to drive his point home, he assured us that Wright's superiors rejected the charges that Hollis was the Superspy. This is hardly surprising, since Wright's most senior superior was Hollis himself!

It was the defector Oleg Gordievsky who, with his inside knowledge of the KGB, had supposedly added a new element to the debate, but his attitude evolved over time. His first comments on the issue were sober and factual, as can be seen in the *Sunday Express* of 9 November, 1986, where Pincher reported that Gordievsky, 'claims the KGB Centre in Moscow never briefed him about the Hollis case or indicated they ever had a spy operating at such a high level.' Thus Gordievsky evidently did not know whether Hollis was a Soviet agent or not: he had merely recorded his ignorance without drawing any conclusions from it. In February 1990, however, he gave a talk on BBC TV in which he took an entirely different line. Unlike most defectors, who are kept under wraps after changing sides, Gordievsky was allowed, and indeed encouraged by the authorities to take part in controversial declarations (which is clear from the extract below). In his television talk Gordievsky emphasised that he was in a position to know everything that went on in the KGB and suggested that the facts about a Soviet Superspy would be widely known in the agency. He insisted that:

> For a period of time in 1981 and 1982, I was practically in charge of the British desk [of the Centre], and during the three years of my time in London, I was a senior KGB officer dealing with Great Britain only. It was not conceivable, really, that there had been such an important agent of the KGB. More than that. If a person like him had been a KGB agent, the people in the First Chief Directorate would have gossiped . . . there would be some indications in the files, in the text books, in the lectures in the KGB schools and so on. But there was no information, and no signs of it at all.

On the most charitable hypothesis, Gordievsky was pulling our leg because the various places in which he looked for a mention of the Superspy are precisely those in which, for any intelligence service intending to operate above nursery level, any such reference would be rigorously suppressed. However there was an apparent reason for his new and emphatic tone. In November 1986, he and Andrew had just got together to collaborate on their 'jointly written' book on the KGB, but the position in February 1990 was quite different. The book was published six months after that date, which means that it must have been virtually finished, and one of its main conclusions was that Hollis was entirely innocent.

A glance at the actual KGB practice as regards highly confidential cases does not back Gordievsky's bland assertions. It is not just that the KGB would never have been so free with delicate information as Gordievsky would have us believe, but that there were serious gaps in his 'unprecedented access' to KGB secrets. For instance, on his own admission he knew nothing about Geoffrey Prime, probably the most important post-war KGB agent in Britain, who provided the Soviets with a stream of ultra-secret SIGINT information from 1968 to 1982 from within GCHQ. Yet in the introduction to *KGB: The Inside Story*, Gordievsky solemnly assures us that, 'the London Residency files indicated that the KGB had no source inside either MI5 or SIS since the arrest of George Blake in 1961.'

Then there is the fiasco of the alleged Soviet penetration of the British SIGINT organisation in Cyprus which Gordievsky is alleged to have reported to MI6 in 1983. On the basis of that information, MI5 descended on the Cyprus base and found as many as eight spies in the Army and Air Force who confessed their sins, adding succulent details of sexual orgies and deviant practices. They were brought back to England, tried, and acquitted, in spite of the vetting of the jury by Special Branch in order to eliminate subversive elements. I suspect the whole affair was a gigantic KGB in-house hoax: that is, a plant whereby suspicions of certain innocent persons were circulated in order to deflect attention from a genuine and more important agent. The operation meant deceiving KGB personnel and thus increasing the possibility of the misinformation being picked up by other agencies. An account of the whole distressing episode can be found in James Rusbridger's *The Intelligence Game* and in an official report of the affair by Sir John Calcutt.

It is significant that both these cases involved SIGINT, which is always regarded as an especially secret matter, and hence they were almost certainly dealt with by a separate KGB directorate to which Gordievsky had no access. It is also probable that special arrangements of which Gordievsky was equally ignorant were made to run the Superspy. In any case, traces of the Superspy end around 1963, just before Hollis retired, at a time when Gordievsky was a raw trainee without access to any sensitive KGB data.

Gordievsky's contribution to the Superspy saga does not end here, for during the final preparation of the manuscript of *KGB: The Inside Story*, his memory suddenly awakened. Whereas in February 1990 he had denied most strenuously that there could have been any high-level penetration agent run by the London Centre, it now occurred to him that there was indeed such an important spy being run from London with the codename ELLI. Unexpectedly, Gordievsky provided the startling information that he had gained access to ELLI's KGB file in 1981 and discovered that he was Leo Long. This 'discovery' was a very shrewd move, because the molehunters, and certainly the public, would have asked who was the spy named by Gouzenko, whose existence had not been called in question even if his exact identity was unknown. Not, of course, that Long fitted the description of ELLI given by defector Gouzenko at all, for he never worked in either MI5 or SIS, but in MI14, and he had left London for a post in Germany soon after the end of the war. The identification of ELLI as Long was therefore greeted with widespread scepticism by intelligence experts. Moreover, and this factor was a crucial advantage, he had retired and was living quietly in England, and could therefore be advised to follow the party line by MI5, the very organisation which had decided not to prosecute him for his activities on behalf of the KGB. In fact Long has been singularly discreet since Andrew's book came out and had I been in a position remotely resembling his, I am certain that I would have been besieged by the usual crowd of reporters. Long has not been subjected to any such ordeal. I pondered the apparent coincidence that the existence of the Long file, almost the only dossier seen by Gordievsky, was only revealed in 1990, and at a very late and highly convenient moment at that?

The extent of the opposition to the Hollis thesis within the Security Service will be clearer if I relate the story of official indifference or sabotage from the very beginning. This takes us back to September 1945 when Igor Gouzenko told the Canadians, and thus the British Security Service, about ELLI, a major Russian agent who had been operational in England at least since 1942.

From the very beginning the MI5 officials dealing with the ELLI case were split into two factions. Most of them preferred to let the evidence gather dust, while a few dissidents attempted, with varying fortunes, to overcome the Establishment's resistance. The main leads were derived from Soviet turncoats. ('There is nothing like a good defector,' as

Arthur Martin once observed to me.) Gouzenko was a GRU cipher clerk who had worked in the Soviet Embassy in Ottawa and went over to the West in September 1945, having been rescued by the Royal Canadian Mounted Police just as some Russian strong-arm men were about to break down the door of his apartment. According to his testimony, Gouzenko had been working on the night shift in the cipher room of the GRU headquarters in Moscow with his old friend Lieutenant Lev Lubimov, and these two often exchanged interesting telegrams, which was strictly forbidden. On one particular night a signal from an agent with the codename ELLI had come in from the Soviet Embassy in London. ELLI held a post in what Gouzenko described as '5 of MI' and apparently was considered so important a source that his telegrams were often taken straight to Stalin. The spy's material would be left in a dead-letter drop beside a grave in an Oxford cemetery in order to avoid the need for frequent meetings with his controller, and thereby reduce the risk of discovery. Gouzenko added that ELLI was able to take the files of Soviet officers in Britain out from his office, which was almost certainly in MI5's temporary base at Blenheim Palace, just outside Oxford, so that these officers could learn what was known about them.

Gouzenko also blew Allan Nunn May's Soviet atomic ring in Canada, and London seemed much more impressed by this news than by the details about ELLI. Philby should have gone out to Ottawa to debrief Gouzenko, since SIS at that time was responsible for counter-intelligence work on Soviet agents abroad, but he had other fish to fry in Istanbul (see page 171). Accordingly, Philby suggested that Hollis should be sent to Canada instead: but Hollis of MI5 who normally only dealt with foreign agents in Britain, did not spend much time with Gouzenko. He devoted most of his report to the atomic spies and made only a few comments on ELLI, almost as if this was matter for a footnote.

Hollis later questioned ELLI's very existence. Yet the whole argument should have been settled by the study of a telegram sent by the KGB in London to Moscow on 19/20 September, 1945, just after Philby had received the first news about Gouzenko's disclosures about ELLI. That message showed the same word count as the British signal from Ottawa to MI5 about Gouzenko's debriefing. This Russian text was not deciphered until 1965, when it was discovered, as reported by Peter Wright in *Spycatcher*, that the immediate reply to it from Moscow was:

'Consent has been obtained from the Chiefs to consult with the neighbours about Stanley's [Philby's] material about their affairs in Canada. Stanley's data is correct.'

The meaning of this message was that the KGB (which operated quite separately from GRU) had been obliged to obtain permission from the Politburo to consult the GRU about their special agent, whose existence had obviously been an extremely secret matter. The telegram confirmed that Philby's information was correct. The clear implication is that the enciphered telegram from London to Moscow was a literal reproduction of the information from Ottawa about ELLI, which Philby, as the folded original showed, had actually handed to his Soviet controller. According to Wright's *Spycatcher*: 'the actual copy of the telegram, when we examined it in the 1960s, was folded into four, with grimy edges, as if it had been placed in an inside pocket, and was initialled off HARP (Philby's initials) two days after he received it.' The only possible interpretation of all this is that ELLI existed and was run by GRU at least from 1942 till 1945. Back in MI5, Hollis's indifference to Gouzenko was widely shared. 'Nobody believed him,' said Evelyn McBarnet, a young MI5 researcher, and Wright reported her comment that: 'They all thought that they had got it wrong. There couldn't be a spy in MI5.'

MI5's lack of interest in Gouzenko's disclosures might have been understandable had it not been for the fact that his report was fully borne out by another Soviet officer at around the same time. This new source was Konstantin Volkov, an NKVD officer acting as the Soviet Vice-Consul in Istanbul. In September 1945, at almost the same moment as Gouzenko was describing the Superspy, he had walked into the British Consulate-General and asked to talk to his opposite number there. For a given sum of money and the guarantee of a safe refuge in the West, he had offered to supply vital information about Soviet agents in British Intelligence. He was asked to provide a shopping list, which he did, and John Reed, a Russian-speaking official, made an overnight translation of the document. The key information was that there were five Soviet agents in British Intelligence and two in the Foreign Office and one of them was 'fulfilling the duties of a Head of Department in British Counterintelligence'. Volkov insisted that his information should not be sent to London by telegraph because he believed that the Foreign Office cipher had been broken by the Soviets. Unfortunately for him, his 'spy list' arrived on Philby's desk at MI6 (where he ran Soviet counter-intelligence). Philby persuaded 'C' to let him go to Istanbul to arrange Volkov's defection, but he delayed long enough for the Soviets to send a plane to Istanbul, where Volkov was kidnapped, bundled aboard, and flown back to Moscow for execution. Philby had some difficulty in explaining away Volkov's sudden disappearance but apparently managed to avoid arousing suspicion. He put the papers away in his safe, where they could not be examined by indiscreet colleagues, or even noted by Registry. It had been, as he admitted in *My Silent War,* 'a very narrow squeak indeed!'

A few years after Volkov's abortive defection, Yuri Rastvorov, a KGB officer based in the Soviet Embassy in Tokyo, claimed that a friend of his named Skripkin had made an offer to defect to the British in 1946, but he first had to return to Moscow to collect his wife. While there, he had been approached by two sham SIS agents, who were really KGB men in disguise. Skripkin had been arrested and executed, and it was later proven that his capture had been the result of a high-level tip-off from London. A copy of two papers about Skripkin, stapled together, had been sent by Naval Intelligence to MI5, and a further copy of these papers, similarly stapled, was later seen by Anatoli Golitsyn at the KGB's Centre. The case had originally been dealt with by Hollis, who had asked a junior official in MI5 to open a file on which he himself took no action.

Other witnesses could be added to this incriminating list. When in late 1961 Golitsyn defected, it was to the Americans, because he knew that the British had been penetrated. He asserted, for example, that the Soviet Embassy in London did not, like other Soviet diplomatic posts, have a security section to check the staff's loyalty because they had such an excellent source in MI5 that they were always warned in advance of any likely defections. Equally serious was his assurance that, in the British Department of the Centre, he had seen a card entitled 'material from the British Security Service' containing an important MI5 technical document dated as late as 1957. The presence in the Centre of MI5 material of that date strongly suggests that the Superspy had been transferred from GRU to the KGB, a point to which attention has never been drawn as far as I know. It is difficult to explain otherwise how the KGB could have obtained such a haul of MI5 material. My guess is that the Superspy's transfer can be explained by the wave of GRU defections in 1945–6 and by the increasingly important role being assumed by the KGB around that time.

The evidence about the Superspy furnished by defectors is thus extensive and concordant, and covers a lengthy period. Moreover, it is supported by the long record of MI5 failures. These included the marked absence of any defectors to Britain and the numerous tip-offs which the Soviet agencies obviously possessed about the movements and plans of British security personnel. Thus the Soviets in Ottawa had prior notice of a visit to Canada in 1944 by the senior MI5 official, Guy Liddell, and Moscow had been warned of an attempt by an SIS-engaged frogman, Commander 'Buster' Crabbe, to measure the pitch of a Russian cruiser's screws during a goodwill visit to Britain by Khrushchev and Bulganin in 1956 (an unidentified headless body was later washed ashore). It has also been reported that numerous English businessmen, when approached by the Soviets to spy, would pretend to accept the offers and then seek to act as double agents, but in every case they were promptly blown.

A most serious indication of Soviet penetration was, as we have seen, the delay in detecting Soviet atomic spies such as Klaus Fuchs, although there were suspicious details in MI5's records which should have alerted the Security Service to him early in his career. No doubt many errors can be explained by incompetence, a desire to maintain a good image with the Americans and generally to protect the agency's good name. Then there was the unwillingness of, for example, the Foreign Office to suspect any of its own members of espionage, preferring to attribute the betrayal of information to known spies such as Blunt and Philby, and to sheer bad luck. But none of these factors can possibly explain away the endless chapter of accidents in MI5's record.

In addition, the evidence given by Blunt in his 1964 confession to MI5 provides grounds for suspicion. He admitted, for example, that he was never asked by the Russians for information from F Division of MI5, which dealt with Soviet agents. He was also instructed by his controller not to ask for personal files on Soviet intelligence officers stationed in Britain. These sensitive documents had been evacuated to MI5's out-station at Blenheim during the war, where Hollis had been moved, along with the rest of his Division, and Hollis had frequently consulted these records. What is even more important, Blunt was not keen to stay in the Security Service after the war, although he liked the work and had been offered a permanent post. He was therefore worried that his controller would press him to stay on, and requested Burgess to intervene with the KGB to allow him to leave. To his surprise and relief, Burgess told him afterwards that there had been no objection to his resignation. This reaction could be taken to mean that the Russians already possessed a highly-placed agent inside MI5.

It would seem therefore that, although there was no material proof of the existence of a Superspy in MI5, the cumulative evidence had become overwhelming. Yet the resistance inside that agency against carrying out an intensive inquiry into the data was unwavering, except on the part of such officers as Peter Wright and Arthur Martin. To summarise: there are three reasons for MI5's tenacious opposition. The first is poor and superficial analysis, often coloured by wishful thinking; the second is the determination of both MI5 and the Foreign Office to refuse to suspect their own staff of treason, and hence to protect them from investigation; and the last would appear to be the sabotage exercised by the supermole himself, especially if he were Hollis – long a senior officer in MI5, then Deputy Director-General, rising finally to the post of Director-General in 1956.

An example of an imperfect analytical approach is the use of the *ad hominem* ploy, that is, abuse of the man rather than the refutation of his arguments. One of the most frequent targets of such an approach was Peter Wright, who led the battle to have the Superspy case thoroughly examined by MI5. It has often been stressed that he betrayed numerous important state secrets in *Spycatcher*, and that he did so for money, of which he was badly in need because he had not received his full pension. In addition to being attacked for selling his country's secrets, Wright was portrayed as having worked too long in counter-espionage, and thus of falling prey to paranoia, as if this were an occupational disease. It is significant, however, that none of these accusations were made against Wright's close collaborator, Arthur Martin, nor against the other dissidents. At most, Martin has been called hot-headed and undisciplined.

These considerations should not affect the strength of Wright's thesis that there was a Superspy in MI5, and that this was Hollis. Moreover, it is difficult to fault his approach, since he consistently pressed for the fullest possible exploitation of SIGINT material. He was always on the look-out for new intercepts to fill the gaps created by Churchill's decision to ban intelligence-gathering operations against Russia till almost the end of the war; and he was constantly pressing GCHQ (Government headquarters) to help him in his research into the identification of Soviet agents.

Wright also shone in the field of linguistic research. He checked both Gouzenko's formula of '5 of MI' and Volkov's shopping list against the views of Russian defectors, and showed that Gouzenko must have been referring to MI5 and not to Section V of SIS. He had Volkov's shopping list re-translated by a GCHQ officer who was not only a fluent Russian speaker but, most importantly, was familiar with the Russian Intelligence Service jargon in use at the time. As a result, the list now read that the important Soviet agent was 'acting head of a section of the British Counter-intelligence *Directorate*', thus placing him definitely in the Security Service (where Philby had never been posted – nor had he ever been an 'acting head'). Wright's concern for scrupulous attention to textual evidence was reflected in a remark which he once made to me about an MI5 statement that 'there was evidence of Mr X's disloyalty' which, after a check, was found to read: 'There was no evidence of Mr X's disloyalty.'

A second victim of the *ad hominem* approach was Gouzenko. It seems that he was a definitely unlovable character, being litigious, eager to exploit his position financially, a compulsive spender, and an alcoholic. But these defects need not weigh against the credibility of his early revelations. Other accusations also have been made in an effort to diminish Gouzenko's importance as a witness, such as the possible confusion of two soviet agents, ELLIE in Ottowa and ELLI in London, but there are other instances of similar duplication by the Soviets. Nigel West's analysis also attempts to defend Hollis, pointing out that ELLI originally placed the Superspy in '5 of MI', but later changed this to MI5. Most experts agree that the term '5 of MI' can in fact only mean MI5. Gouzenko was only a cipher clerk and hence was not familiar with the intricacies of the British Intelligence organisation. He was probably even unaware that SIS (MI6) had a counter-espionage section, Section V. Moreover, it is very rare for SIS ever to be referred to as MI6 by the Russians, whereas MI5 is in common use. In any case, Gouzenko, noting that the newspapers always referred to that agency when discussing his case, quickly corrected his awkward terminology by using the current description.

The reason for the molehunters' emphasis on this point was their determination to show that the Superspy was Kim Philby, but he does not fit the bill. In 1942, which is the period to which Gouzenko referred in his disclosures of 1945, Philby was head of the Iberian branch in Section V of SIS, and therefore is hardly likely to have had direct access (as ELLI was alleged to have had) to files on Russian KGB officials, least of all in Britain, for Philby only dealt with enemy agents abroad. Moreover, he was run by the KGB, whereas ELLI was, at least initially, a GRU man. And, to conclude the argument, Philby was posted abroad in 1946 and sacked in 1951 whereas, according to Golitsyn's evidence, ELLI's hand was visible at least until 1957. In the same context, it is relevant that Blunt, for his part, left MI5 in 1945.

Nigel West goes even further in *Molehunt*. He queried Wright's assertion that the two crucial KGB telegrams (London–Moscow and Moscow–London) referred to earlier applied to ELLI. He was convinced that the second of these signals constituted a warning from Moscow to Allan Nunn May, the atomic scientist in Canada denounced by Gouzenko, who intended to return to Britain in October 1945 where British security planned to trap him at a meeting with his controller. Nothing in this comparison fits. The telegrams were exchanged during the week of 20 to 27 September and the two high priority telegrams discussed here have, moreover, been shown to be a message to Moscow and the Centre's reply. Moscow, to recapitulate, confirmed the accuracy of Philby's information, including the codename and the fact that ELLI worked for GRU. In any case, it is out of the question that a KGB telegram would be sent to London containing a warning for a GRU agent.

West tries to get round this difficulty by suggesting that, as the result of a 'shake-up', there may have been a merger between the KGB and the GRU's operations, but there is not the slightest evidence to warrant such a deduction. A takeover by the GRU of some of the chores of the Comintern is adduced by West in support of his theory, but that is quite a different matter from the union of the two main spy agencies. The Comintern was regarded by the Russians as small beer, if not as actually suspect. West argues that Hollis's deputy, Mitchell, up to his retirement in September 1963, is a better candidate for the role of the Superspy. As we have seen, Mitchell was interrogated by MI5 internally, but nothing could be proved against him and, later, he was cleared by a Cabinet inquiry in 1974 which was directed to investigate the whole question of high-level KGB penetration. West argues that

Mitchell's benevolent attitude towards Philby, and the numerous errors in the briefs prepared by him, give grounds for suspicion. My own feeling is that Graham Mitchell was misguided, like many others, in his support for Philby, and that both this and the errors in documents drafted by him are due in part to incompetence, but mainly to a desire to gloss over MI5's mistakes in order to present a suitable image of the agency to Parliament and the public.

The second obstacle to discovering the identity of the Superspy was the reluctance of MI5 to go into the question in any depth. This hesitancy can be explained on three grounds. One is the obvious difficulty for the staff in investigating the allegation that its Director-General was a foreign agent; the other is the English public school complicity which, with mafia-like solidarity, pervaded MI5 at a time when its members were mostly recruited by personal recommendation by and within a social élite. Their haunts were such select West End clubs as Boodle's and White's, where many of the key decisions were taken and unofficial meetings were held. Much the same observation can be made about the Foreign Office, though the stiff entrance examinations tended to dilute its social purity. However, it still regarded its staff as 'the family' with a marked protective exclusiveness. It is hardly surprising that the two main dissidents in MI5, Wright and Martin, did not go to public schools, which, with Oxbridge, provide the leaders of the still firmly class-structured England.

The last, and perhaps the most obvious obstacle to clearing up the mystery, is the pressure or sabotage coming from the Superspy himself. As we have seen, there are in fact very strong indications of direct interference by Hollis in this sense. His casual attitude toward Gouzenko's disclosures about ELLI and his subsequent action in pigeon-holing the case are difficult to dismiss as mere lightheartedness. Even worse was the tip-off leading to the capture and execution in 1946 of the would-be defector Skripkin, which betrayal Wright traces back to Hollis. Many other leaks on equally serious matters can be attributed to him and among the cases listed as suspicious by Wright is that of the atomic spy, Klaus Fuchs.

Equally grave is the evidence of constant indifference, and often opposition, to anything connected with the Superspy investigation. Significant leads were not followed up, and officers such as Martin who pressed for action were penalised. Martin himself was exiled to Malaya from 1954 to 1959, and he was later dismissed at short notice by Hollis and snapped up by SIS. It was not until the latter year that steps were taken finally to investigate Soviet penetration when a body codenamed the FLUENCY Working Party was set up with six members, three drawn from MI5 and three from SIS. Both Wright and Martin were on it, and Martin remained a member even after his transfer to SIS. According to Peter Wright, all the members believed that Hollis was the culprit. Hollis himself took no special interest in this body, and the pace of advance was reportedly very slow, reflecting a tendency to avoid coming to grips with the three main defectors who had reported on the Superspy. In any case, Hollis was on the eve of his retirement and, if Wright's account of his last interview is to be believed, Hollis was vague and evasive in the talk between the two men. 'I don't really recollect Skripkin, to be honest . . .' he said. 'I don't think you've got Volkov right,' he added. Hollis even accepted Philby's misinformation that Volkov's 'acting head of a branch of MI5' was Philby himself, which is quite absurd because, as already mentioned, he was never an acting head of anything, and was never in MI5. Philby's comments were made long after he had been blown and his subsequent defection when he still had every interest in deflecting MI5's attention from any undiscovered Soviet agents.

Nor did matters change much when Martin Furnival Jones, the new Director-General, took over from Hollis in 1965. Progress in the FLUENCY Working Party continued to be slow. At one meeting, Wright says that Furnival Jones described the charges against Hollis as 'grotesque', flinging the papers being examined on to his desk. The attitude of Furnival Jones's deputy, Anthony Simkins, was also fiercely negative. Still, the suspicions about Hollis mounted steadily, but in 1970 when he was brought back from retirement for interrogation, he was treated with every consideration, and in the process certain possibilities of cracking him were not exploited. Even so, he proved unconvincing. He maintained his innocence and shrugged off Gouzenko, Volkov and Skripkin just as rapidly as in his talk with Wright five years earlier. He doubted whether Gouzenko was reliable, and whether ELLI had really existed, despite the exchange of telegrams between the KGB in London and Moscow Centre exhumed in 1965. Even so, there was evidently no point in bringing him to a public scandal. He would simply have dug his toes in, and the consequences of such a fiasco on the Security Service would have been boundless.

Things seemed to have come to an impasse, but feeling among the rebels in MI5 ran so high in 1974 that a former FLUENCY committee spokesman decided to take the matter up directly with the Prime Minister's Office. It turned out, according to Wright, that Harold Wilson, who headed the Labour Government at the time, was virtually uninformed about the case. He therefore decided that a recently retired Cabinet Secretary, Sir Burke Trend, should carry out a secret investigation, but Trend's terms of reference were not to sit in judgement on Hollis. He was only to ascertain that all the evidence available had been fairly examined and that there had been no manipulation of the data. The Intelligence chiefs and those Whitehall mandarins in on the secret seemed, as always, anxious to see Hollis cleared, and it was decided that he should be regarded as innocent if no further evidence emerged against him.

At one point, Wright had a talk with Trend about the scandal and, if his version of the meeting is accurate, it brings out the ex-Cabinet Secretary's unfamiliarity with Intelligence matters, despite his undoubted brilliance as an administrator. At least Trend was impressed by the 'uncanny' coincidence of the allegations made by Gouzenko and Volkov, but he insisted that these accounts were very old, as if their credibility and relevance could thereby be discounted. 'Golitsyn,' said Trend, 'did not lead anywhere.' Clearly for Trend, in the absence of a name and address for the Superspy, the evidence of the various defectors must be discarded. He added that Wright's decision to have Volkov's shopping list re-examined 'altered the thrust of the allegation' in the original document, to which Wright replied, correctly, that every text had to be carefully looked at. In fact Wright's check definitely had served to clarify Volkov's information. Trend added that 'there was no follow-up on Gouzenko', but this was due to the lack of intercepts and to GCHQ's inability to decipher much of the new material which was obtained in the mid-1940s. Yet the key information about ELLI *had* been confirmed fully in 1965 by the decrypted telegrams of September 1945 passed between Moscow and London. Trend also pointed out that Hollis showed no signs of an ideological Communist background, overlooking the absence of any such traces in the early days of Blake, whose conversion was only brought about by skilful interrogation by the KGB in Korea. Certainly Trend took no account of Hollis's political sophistication, as recently revealed by his biographer, William West.

The weight of evidence is that Trend returned a verdict of what in Scotland would have been 'Not proven' – the impression being that Hollis had been cleared.

The findings of the Trend Report were not made public until 1981, and then only when they were disclosed by Pincher in *Their Trade Is Treachery*. Contesting his accuracy, Mrs Thatcher made a declaration in Parliament which was drafted by the Cabinet Office in conjunction with MI5. This document has not worn well, for it gives the impression that the existence of a Superspy in MI5 was by no means certain, and that she thought the evidence suggested that hostile penetration had been limited to 'the last years of the war'. She went on to assert that none of the leads to the Superspy 'identified Sir Roger or pointed specifically or wholly in his direction. Each of them could also be taken as pointing to Philby or Blunt.' This last part of her statement does not stand up to analysis because, as already noted, Blunt left MI5 in 1945, and Philby was posted abroad the following year. As Pincher has pointed out, 'several of the leads that made the FLUENCY Committee suspicious occurred long after these dates,' that is, not just in a wartime context as Mrs Thatcher alleged. The whole issue was paraphrased much more accurately by *The Times* leader which observed that 'Mrs Thatcher has now officially revealed that there were serious professional suspicions about Sir Roger Hollis which do not seem to have been dispelled, but merely disposed of, as it were, by majority verdict.'

Margaret Thatcher's virtual exoneration of Hollis may have relieved the Establishment, but it left the public exasperated because no explanation had been offered for MI5's failures in the 1940s and 1950s, short of a remarkable degree of inefficiency. Andrew's arguments were, generally speaking, accepted uncritically: and his reviewers, in the UK and in America, failed to point out the basic fallacy in his treatment of Hollis. Accordingly, concern about the Superspy died down, and even Chapman Pincher, most critical of the molehunters, did not feel that he could go further than his letter to *The Times* of 2 November, 1990 in which he wrote: 'The evidence against Hollis . . . cannot be attributed to Cairncross, or convincingly to anyone else and still stands.' Arthur Martin writing from his retirement sums up the whole question fairly in the following eloquent letter to *The Times* published on 19 July, 1984:

My recollection is that while Hollis fitted the circumstantial evidence more closely than any other candidate, the case against him was not conclusive. It was the evidence of continued penetration of the service after Blunt retired in 1945 until at least the early 1960s which carried complete conviction among those working on the case. When in 1969 the interrogation of Hollis failed to produce a conclusive answer, it would have been normal practice to continue the search but to widen its scope: if it was not Hollis who was it? Instead, the investigating team was disbanded, and the case allowed to lapse. It was that decision, I believe, which led to a decade of unease which still festers today. For it is inconceivable that the Security Service would have allowed an investigation to lapse if similar evidence of penetration had been discovered in any other department of government. It has been suggested from time to time that yet another official inquiry into the case should be made. In my view this would be pointless. No amount of re-examination can resolve the case: only new evidence will do that. New evidence, if it comes, will be by chance or renewed Security Service effort.

My personal contact with Martin left me with a great appreciation of his capacity. It may not be possible to fool all the people all the time, but, given the right circumstances and the right accomplices in high places, almost anything is possible. Indeed, the questions concerning the Superspy have never been answered, at least not in public. I have no doubt that new evidence and further disclosures will reveal facts at least corresponding to the truth, and I would personally welcome such a development. British Intelligence would gain from a dose of 'perestroika', and the British public would then be in a position to discount misleading reports and make an informed judgement.

FOURTEEN

Je Ne Regrette Rien

'Every spy,' it is said, 'feels that he is a special case.' Strangely enough, I do too, for my involvement with the KGB was not animated by the usual ideological reasons or financial motives. It will also be difficult to reconcile my 'career' with the prevailing cliché of the standard 'spy' story, for I was perpetually out of my milieu in the twilight world of espionage, always a loner but always a survivor. Characteristic of my Calvinist upbringing, I have constantly felt the need to explain my actions and, in particular, to give the reasons for them for I would rather be stamped as unconventional than confused. I have also been impelled by the scholar's determination to see clearly into a complex issue. I therefore believe my story should be accepted as true since my statements can be verified and my actions given perspective when placed in a historical context.

Although I am a very private person, avoiding the limelight whether flattering or critical, and not given to introspection, writing this frank account of my life for public scrutiny has not been a painful experience; rather has it been an illuminating journey. Far from finding it a strain, I experienced an increasing sense of pleasure in penetrating the smoke-screen of lies and errors about me, as the various pieces of the puzzle fell into place. Mud has already been thrown at me, and some of it will inevitably stick, but I have no reason to feel ashamed of anything I have done. I never worked for the enemy, but for a potential or actual ally; and I do not feel I have reason to regret my actions since I was never a *vendu* who sold information at any time to anyone. Had I been pressed, moreover, to commit actions I did not approve of, or obtain information which I would be unwilling to provide, I would have dug my toes in and refused.

As for the actual mechanics of my recruitment, I was caught in a clever KGB trap: but none of the devices so often deployed were used – no threatened revelation of compromising sexual involvement, no threat to reveal a secret surreptitiously discovered, no direct attempt at blackmail. How other people of my background and age at that time would have reacted in those circumstances, I cannot say, but my decision (made at the age of 23) to deliver secret information to a foreign power was meant to last only for the duration and was taken despite the existence of a Communist régime in Russia and not because of it. I always remained master of the information I passed, excluding anything which did not concern the Russians directly or involved specifically British interests. Thus, although I would have preferred to suppress them altogether, I regard my short stint for the KGB before 1941 and my continued association with them after 1945, as the price I have had to pay for my decision in 1937. In the same way, I held on during the dismal period when Russia was allied with Nazi Germany as an act of faith. My goal was to work for Britain's survival in a world where the balance of power was moving sharply against us as Hitler re-armed and Chamberlain surrendered to him one power position after another. Even after the German invasion of Russia in 1941, my involvement was not a question of sympathy for the sufferings of the Russian people (though I was certainly not indifferent to them) but was based on a simple calculation of strategic factors. In other words, the premise for my action were of an essentially practical character.

Some readers may find it inexplicable that a significant section of the intellectual élite in England should have, in the 1930s, sympathised with the Marxist/Communist creed and even, in a few cases, carried their convictions to the point of engaging in espionage for the KGB. My flirtation with Communism at Cambridge should, one critic reproached me, have alerted me to the danger of a KGB trap, and I was criticised for my inability to scent the essence of the KGB on my academic doorstep at Trinity: but I had no difficulty in retorting that MI5, which was much better equipped than I to effect such a discovery, had also failed completely to detect the odour of the KGB.

I have sometimes asked myself what lessons, if any, I learned. The most obvious moral is that it is impossible with any accuracy to predict the future. Things never turn out as one expects, especially in the shadowy world of Intelligence. I never could have predicted the

Molotov-Ribbentrop Pact and I was surprised by the actual collapse of France, though I had envisioned it mentally for quite a long time. Nor did I anticipate the utter change in Anglo–Soviet relations after the war. On espionage matters I was in the dark most of the time, and the unexpected offer of immunity that I received, thanks to MI5's fear of the exposure of Blunt after 1964, came as a windfall, just as the brazen attempt by Christopher Andrew to portray me as a more sinister figure than I am came as a shock.

In reality, both the KGB and MI5 have treated me in much the same manner. They both showed a disregard for the principles their agencies are trusted to defend. Their contempt for the truth has become part of the methods of their professional self-defence, and the rights of the accused do not exist. In this, MI5 does not seem much better than the spies they are supposed to deal with. The Security Service offered me, of its own accord, immunity if I kept quiet, which I did, even after Chapman Pincher had splashed my activities, grievously distorted, over his pages. I was thus exposed to the full blast of press attacks without a means to respond. But I felt my obligation was not just to MI5 but to Britain, as I have never wanted to undermine her. After I had asked MI5 to be allowed to defend myself against unjustified innuendoes, I was reminded about my duty of confidentiality and of the Official Secrets Act.

The KGB has also played a public relations game. When Modin incorrectly stated that he had reactivated me in 1948, that I met him after 1952, and that I had also met other KGB representatives in France or in Italy, he was simply trying to make the KGB record look a little better, since they were embarrassed at having dropped me like a hot potato in 1951. Their image is certainly more important to them than the truth. For a time, not wanting to break with the tradition of appearing to remain loyal to agents who are still alive, they gave only the bare facts about me, playing down the whole affair. Unfortunately their silence had the opposite effect, and I would certainly have preferred more access to their records.

MI5, which has perfected the art of defending itself against internal or public challenges, was guilty on other scores besides the refusal to allow me to speak out. They well knew that I was not the Fifth Man or the first atomic spy, and they never questioned me on either charge. Why would Gordievsky confide his knowledge to Dr Andrew instead of to the Security Service, or work with him without the consent of his SIS handlers? Gordievsky had long since been debriefed by both British Intelligence agencies so I cannot believe MI5's legal adviser was serious in asking me to spell out Andrew's name when I telephoned to report his intention to publish his book.

Of course, bigger interests were involved and my story points to the moral that MI5 should be made even more accountable. This may not eliminate the main abuses but it will afford a shield against the tendencies of an agency which has until now felt all powerful to act in a completely arbitrary fashion in defence, not of the national interests, but of its own image. If it is argued that the agency would thus be hobbled in the exercise of its duties, the reply is obvious. They could not make a worse showing than they have done in the last fifty years, when most of their successes are due to sheer chance and to signals intelligence, provided by other agencies.

This special world of Intelligence was well understood by Graham Greene, who had an unusual insight into the politics of espionage as revealed in his marvellous book *The Human Factor*. Loyalty and support for his friends were two other facets of his generous nature. He certainly surpassed himself in his defence of me when I was labelled the Fifth Man. Though terminally ill and subjected to constant blood transfusions, he remained untiring in his support for me. His letter of recommendation to the French government gave me great pleasure: I particularly admire the work he has done in his translations and critical studies on Molière and other French classics whom the English are too lazy to read without assistance. I think France owes him a great debt for his work in this field.' At my last meeting with him in his Antibes apartment, shortly before he left for Switzerland in 1990, we discussed Philby's rather sad end ('What a fuss about Kim,' he had written after his friend had escaped to Russia in 1963). I was greatly comforted by his comments on my case and his encouragement for me to tell my real story once the Russians had come out with their version. (Philby's real story, for instance, may never be known.) Whatever his convictions, I always remember Graham as one of the kindliest, most unaffected and most human persons I have ever met. These qualities have to a great extent been pressed into the background by his towering greatness as a writer. Many of his admirers felt that if anyone deserved a Nobel Prize, it was he. It is consoling to think that such considerations never occurred to him.

There is at least one Russian proverb with which I am in agreement: 'Don't be born handsome. Don't be born rich. Be born lucky.' My one-time master, Lord Hankey, used to say that the most practical criterion in war was whether an officer was lucky, and not what his tactical skill or bravery was. I have, I think, had more than the ordinary measure of good fortune in twice escaping death by a direct hit during the war. I have usually lived in beautiful cities abroad, had enjoyable jobs and my personal life has been of the happiest. My writings have been appreciated by illustrious colleagues and published in academic journals. But my personal drama is replete with irony, and events were often guided by chance. My first interrogation by MI5 resulted in my resignation from the Treasury, but enabled me at last to break with the KGB and move to Italy where I spent many happy years. The 'important papers' I had lent to Burgess, however, had not been associated in any way with the KGB and I had been completely unaware of his KGB connections. After my confession in 1964 I had expected the heavens to fall, but, on the contrary, sailed out on Blunt's capacious coat tails – the man who had talent-spotted me in the first place. Lastly, the circumstances created by Andrew's book impelled me to dig up a part of my life which I had relegated to limbo and, contrary to MI5's wishes, to speak out. It would never otherwise have occurred to me to write my memoirs, for I have no exaggerated idea about the importance of my life.

I would never have approached the KGB of my own accord, though I would certainly have linked up with a Churchillian party had such existed in 1937. Moreover, had Churchill been in power at that period before the 1939 war, and not a voice in the wilderness, my whole approach to the Russian question would have been different. Having spent much of my early years on the continent – where fascism was an integral part of everyday life – I could not adopt an insular and complaisant view of the events leading up to Munich. The only answer to the threat of German aggression was, I felt, re-armament and the formation of a firm military alliance between Britain, France, Czechoslovakia and Russia: I hold these same views today.

But I suppose I was more lucky than brave, and if my motives were pure, they were not enough. I survived, in no small measure because I handled my case with a mixture of evasiveness and patience. Had I reported everything dutifully to my superiors at the beginning, I would have been well and truly crushed; and the Allies would have been deprived of my one important contribution to the Allied victory – the defeat of the German armies at the Battle of Kursk in 1943.

Index